GAMBLING WITH OTHER PEOPLE'S MONEY

# Gambling with Other People's Money

*How Perverse Incentives Caused the Financial Crisis*

RUSS ROBERTS

HOOVER INSTITUTION PRESS

STANFORD UNIVERSITY    STANFORD, CALIFORNIA

*With its eminent scholars and world-renowned library and archives,*
*the Hoover Institution seeks to improve the human condition*
*by advancing ideas that promote economic opportunity and*
*prosperity, while securing and safeguarding peace for America and all mankind.*
*The views expressed in its publications are entirely those of the authors and do not*
*necessarily reflect the views of the staff, officers, or Board of Overseers of the Hoover*
*Institution.*

*www.hoover.org*

**Hoover Institution Press Publication No. 692**

Hoover Institution at Leland Stanford Junior University,
Stanford, California 94305-6003

Hoover Institution Press assumes no responsibility for the persistence or
accuracy of URLs for external or third-party Internet websites referred to in
this publication, and does not guarantee that any content on such websites is,
or will remain, accurate or appropriate.

First printing 2019
25   24   23   22   21   20   19       8   7   6   5   4   3   2

Manufactured in the United States of America

The paper used in this publication meets the minimum Requirements of the
American National Standard for Information Sciences—Permanence of Paper
for Printed Library Materials, ANSI/NISO Z39.48-1992. ⊖

Cataloging-in-Publication Data is available from the Library of Congress.
ISBN: 978-0-8179-2185-9 (pbk. : alk. paper)
ISBN: 978-0-8179-2186-6 (epub)
ISBN: 978-0-8179-2187-3 (mobi)
ISBN: 978-0-8179-2188-0 (PDF)

# CONTENTS

*Someday you guys are going to have to tell me how we ended up with a system like this. I know this is not the time to test them and put them through failure, but we're not doing something right if we're stuck with these miserable choices.*

—President George W. Bush, talking to Ben Bernanke and Hank Paulson when told it was necessary to bail out AIG

*The curious task of economics is to demonstrate to men how little they really know about what they imagine they can design.*

—F. A. Hayek, *The Fatal Conceit*

# ACKNOWLEDGMENTS

My understanding of the issues in this book was greatly enhanced and influenced by numerous conversations with Sam Eddins, Dino Falaschetti, Arnold Kling, and Paul Romer. I am grateful to them for their time and patience. I also wish to thank Mark Adelson, Karl Case, Guy Cecala, William Cohan, Stephan Cost, Amy Fontinelle, Zev Fredman, Paul Glashofer, David Gould, Daniel Gressel, Heather Hambleton, Avi Hofman, Brian Hooks, Ed Pinto, Rob Raffety, Daniel Rebibo, Gary Stern, John Taylor, Jeffrey Weiss, and Jennifer Zambone for their comments and helpful conversations on various aspects of financial and monetary policy. I received helpful feedback from presentations to the Hoover Institution's Working Group on Global Markets, George Mason University's Department of Economics, and the Mercatus Center's Financial Markets Working Group. I am grateful for research assistance from Benjamin Klutsey and Ryan Langrill. None of the above bears any responsibility for any errors in this book.

# PREFACE TO THE 2019 EDITION

The Financial Crisis of 2008 has spawned thousands of pages about what caused the worst economic events since the Great Depression. Most explanations blame the crisis on either government regulation or government deregulation. Either government forced private sector banks and financial institutions to extend credit to risky borrowers or the removal of government oversight allowed greed to run amok via risky loans, corrupted credit ratings, and complex mortgage-backed securities and derivatives that were poorly understood.

I find these stories fundamentally unsatisfying. Yes, government forced banks to extend mortgages to homebuyers who normally would not have qualified for a mortgage. But banks seemed eager to make these loans, including financial institutions who were not facing government mandates. Yes, government reduced oversight which allowed banks to make increasingly risky loans. But why would banks lend recklessly and put their survival at risk?

These narratives ignore how government bailouts in the decades preceding the crisis encouraged risky lending using borrowed money. While there has been deregulation, government is still heavily involved in financial markets. The problem is that government policy is only free-market when there are gains to be made. When there are losses, government policy is socialist, creating a safety net for some of the richest people in human history. The result is crony capitalism masquerading as the real thing.

At the heart of the story I tell in this book is a simple idea—if you don't think you're going to pay for your mistakes, you'll make more of them.

I try to show how government policies caused investors to believe they would be protected from their mistakes. My claim is that government's treatment of financial institutions in the decades preceding the crisis distorted the natural feedback loops of profit and loss that balance risk-taking with prudence. The result was a lot more risk-taking and a lot less prudence. Most of the players felt they had little skin in the game. In almost all cases, the bailouts came as expected, confirming the feeling that risk was low.

By removing the downside risk, especially for creditors—investors who lend money expecting a fixed amount of income in return—government policy allowed investors to use borrowed money rather than their own. As a result, many people were able to play with other people's money—the homeowners who financed their homes with little or nothing down, the mortgage companies who sold risky mortgages to others, the financial institutions that sold bundled mortgages to investors, and even the investors who bought those financial instruments. Ultimately, the only participant unable to place the risk of these activities onto someone else was the taxpayer. And even taxpayers were able to avoid some of the pain because government debt imposed those costs on future taxpayers.

It is tempting then, to blame Washington, not Wall Street for the mess that followed. Some so-called free-marketers defend bankers, arguing that they merely responded to the incentives created by public policy. But Wall Street is not a passive observer of the political scene or the regulatory environment. Wall Street executives sit on the board of the Federal Reserve, fund political campaigns, and chat on the phone with the secretary of the Treasury. Wall Street lobbied relentlessly for the incentives that they responded to. Yes, the financial sector responded to the rules of the game. But the financial sector helps write the rules of the game.

This book was originally published in 2010 in essay form while I was a professor of economics at George Mason University and a scholar at George Mason's Mercatus Center. The only thing I have changed of significance in this version is to correct an error: Washington Mutual and not just Lehman Brothers was allowed to go bankrupt.

The main thing that has changed in my thinking since 2010 is an increased skepticism about attempts to explain the complexity of economic outcomes and an increased awareness of our human tendency to adopt narratives we find pleasing. Certainly, many factors beyond those identified here contributed to the crisis. But the influence of past bailouts that I focus on here has been insufficiently appreciated, partly because of the challenge of measuring expectations with any precision and partly because it's a narrative that doesn't fall neatly into the standard narratives that the crisis was caused by too much regulation or too little.

What I have tried to do here is collect the evidence that is available on how past bailouts influenced decision making. Is the evidence persuasive? Like much social science research, there is an inherent complexity in the events preceding 2008 that is probably unresolvable. But I hope I have made clear in this book that the decades before the crisis were not some free-market paradise.

The fact of government involvement via bailouts is surprisingly easy to forget. Alan Greenspan, in testimony before Congress in the aftermath of the crisis, conceded that the collapse of financial markets had caused him to question his principles, a reference presumably to the self-regulating nature of markets.

Greenspan conveniently forgot that he himself had been an important distorter of market forces that might otherwise have led to more stability. In addition to monetary policy that pushed interest rates down when the stock market was struggling (the so-called Greenspan put), he orchestrated the rescue of Long-Term Capital Management. Despite his reputation as a free-market ideologue, Greenspan testified before Congress in 1995 urging the rescue of the American banks who had lent money to Mexico:

> This program, in my judgment, is the least worst of the various initiatives that present themselves as possible solutions to a very unsettling international

financial problem. Our concerns are not so much
with potential losses to the US taxpayer, which we
believe will be minimized, but with what economists
call moral hazard—when the active involvement of an
external guarantor distorts the incentives perceived
by investors . . . I see no viable alternative to the type
of program that is being presented to the Congress
if the financial erosion is to be stanched before it
threatens to become a wider problem.

Greenspan was only a free-market ideologue when
it helped Wall Street. Otherwise, he believed in intervention.

Some observers have pointed out that investors are
capable of stupid decision making even without the
promise of a bailout. You don't need the expectation of
a bailout for people to follow the herd when asset prices
are rising, to make bad decisions, and to lose all their
money. So past bailouts may not have been relevant to the
crisis of 2008. Perhaps. But even if you believe that people
ignored the prospect of being bailed out, it's important to
understand the effects and costs of bailouts even when
people don't anticipate them.

Letting people lose their money has to be a crucial
centerpiece of any financial system. Investors who make
imprudent decisions and get wiped out no longer get to
allocate scarce capital through imprudent risk-taking
in the future. As Nassim Nicholas Taleb has observed,
this pruning of bad investors improves decision making
even if people are blind to the riskiness of their decisions.
Letting bad investors lose all their money means that the
worst decision makers are sent home. Letting losers go

bankrupt improves the allocation of capital even if the players fail to notice the incentives.

Bailouts keep bad decision makers alive to play another day. Bailouts encourage banks to be entangled with other banks—the systemic risk that allow banks to impose risks on other banks. That entanglement justifies future bailouts. Capital gets allocated poorly because the worst decision makers remain at the table. Bailouts encourage excessive leverage—the other people's money that reduces the incentive for prudence for those who are paying attention. So even if you discount the importance of bailouts as an underlying cause of the crisis, they still distort financial markets in very unhealthy ways.

An important issue I did not address in the original version of this book is the net impact of bailouts on taxpayers. As of June 2018, ProPublica estimates that the bailouts of over 900 financial institutions have resulted in about $90 billion in net revenue for the government through interest, dividends, paybacks, and sales of government-acquired assets. This has led some to conclude that the bailouts were costless or even profitable. Such calculations ignore the opportunity cost of government funds—that the money being lent out at below market rates could have been used elsewhere.

But the more important point is that the cost to the taxpayer is not the true cost of a bailout. The true cost is the disruption of the incentives of profit and loss with the resulting misallocation of capital. I believe the bailouts of the past encouraged reckless investment in the housing sector. There should have been investments in other things—more efficient cars, better medical devices, or whatever investors would have chosen besides housing. Instead, we got more and bigger houses. That's a bad exchange. That those investments in other things and subsequent human benefits did not occur is the real cost of the bailouts of the past.

Bailouts have another cost—they undermine the credibility of democracy. They tell the citizens that some people—the politically powerful—are worthy of a do-over, while others must suffer the consequences of their actions. Bailouts are the symptoms of crony capitalism. I prefer the real thing—a system where everyone plays by the same rules of profit and loss.

Despite the passage of Dodd-Frank, it is widely believed that we have done little to eliminate the expectation of future bailouts for large financial institutions. That allows the largest financial institutions to continue to gamble implicitly with taxpayer money. My hope is that if the public understands how bailouts encourage excessive borrowing and the imprudent allocation of capital, politicians will be less eager to allow investors to escape without paying a price when the next crisis arises.

I am grateful to the Mercatus Center for the support I received in writing this essay and the freedom they gave me to pursue whatever explanations and causes I found plausible. And I am grateful to the Hoover Institution and the Hoover Institution Press for support and for this book.

# INTRODUCTION

B eginning in the mid-1990s, home prices in many American cities began a decade-long climb that proved to be an irresistible opportunity for investors.

Along the way, a lot of people made a great deal of money. But by the end of the first decade of the twenty-first century, too many of these investments turned out to be much riskier than many people had thought. Homeowners lost their houses, financial institutions imploded, and the entire financial system was in turmoil.[1]

How did this happen? Whose fault was it?

A 2009 study by the Congressional Research Service identified 26 causes of the crisis.[2] The Financial Crisis Inquiry Commission is studying 22 different potential causes of the crisis.[3] In the face of such complexity, it is tempting to view the housing crisis and subsequent financial crisis as a once-in-a-century coincidental conjunction of destructive forces. As Alan Schwartz, Bear Stearns's last CEO, put it, "We all [messed] up. Government. Rating agencies. Wall Street. Commercial banks. Regulators. Investors. Everybody."[4]

In this commonly held view, the housing market collapse and the subsequent financial crisis were a perfect storm of private and public mistakes. People bought houses they couldn't afford. Firms bundled the mortgages for these houses into complex securities. Investors and financial institutions bought these securities thinking they were less risky than they actually were. Regulators who might have prevented the mess were asleep on the job. Greed and hubris ran amok. Capitalism ran amok.

To those who accept this narrative, the lesson is clear. As Paul Samuelson put it,

> And today we see how utterly mistaken was the Milton Friedman notion that a market system can regulate itself. We see how silly the Ronald Reagan slogan was that government is the problem, not the solution. This prevailing ideology of the last few decades has now been reversed. Everyone understands now, on the contrary, that there can be no solution without government.[5]

The implication is that we need to reject unfettered capitalism and embrace regulation. But Wall Street and the housing market are hardly unfettered. Yes, deregulation and mis-regulation contributed to the crisis, but mainly because public policy over the last three decades has distorted the natural feedback loops of profit and loss. As Milton Friedman liked to point out, capitalism is a profit and loss system. The profits encourage risk-taking. The losses encourage prudence. When taxpayers absorb the losses, the distorted result is reckless and imprudent risk-taking.

A different mistake is to hold Wall Street and the financial sector blameless, for after all, investment bankers and other financial players were just doing what they are supposed to—maximizing profits and responding to the incentives and the rules of the game. But Wall Street helps write the rules of the game. Wall Street staffs the Treasury Department. Washington staffs Fannie Mae and Freddie Mac. In the week before the AIG bailout that put $14.9 billion into the coffers of Goldman Sachs, Treasury secretary and former Goldman Sachs CEO Hank Paulson called Goldman Sachs CEO Lloyd Blankfein at least 24 times.[6] I don't think they were talking about how their kids were doing.

This book explores how changes in the rules of the game—some made for purely financial motives, some made for more altruistic reasons—created the mess we are in.

The most culpable policy has been the systematic encouragement of imprudent borrowing and lending. That encouragement came not from capitalism or markets, but from crony capitalism, the mutual aid society where Washington takes care of Wall Street and Wall Street returns the favor.[7] Over the last three decades, public policy has systematically reduced the risk of making bad loans to risky investors. Over the last three decades, when large financial institutions have gotten into trouble, the government has almost always rescued their bondholders and creditors. These policies have created incentives to both borrow and lend recklessly.

When large financial institutions get in trouble, equity holders (stockholders) are typically wiped out or made to suffer significant losses when share values plummet. The punishment of equity holders is usually thought to mitigate the potential for moral hazard created by the rescue of creditors. But it does not. It merely masks the role of creditor rescues in creating perverse incentives for risk-taking.

The expectation by creditors that they might be rescued allows financial institutions to substitute borrowed money for their own capital even as they make riskier and riskier investments. Because of the large amounts of leverage—the use of debt rather than equity—executives can more easily generate short-term profits that justify large compensation. While executives endure some of the pain if short-term gains become losses in the long run, the downside risk to the decision makers turns out to be surprisingly small, while the upside gains can be enormous. Taxpayers ultimately bear much of the downside risk. Until we recognize the pernicious incentives created by the persistent rescue of creditors, no regulatory reform is likely to succeed.

Almost all of the lenders who financed bad bets in the housing market paid little or no cost for their recklessness. Their expectations of rescue were confirmed. But the expectation of creditor rescue was not the only factor in the crisis. As I will show, housing policy, tax policy, and monetary policy all contributed, particularly in their interaction. Though other factors—the repeal of the Glass-Steagall Act, predatory lending, changes in capital requirements, and so on—made things worse, I focus on creditor rescue, housing policy, tax policy, and monetary policy because without these policies and their interaction, the crisis would not have occurred at all. And among causes, I focus on creditor rescue and housing policy because they are the most misunderstood.

In the United States, we like to believe we are a capitalist society based on individual responsibility. But we are what we do. Not what we say we are. Not what we wish to be. But what we do. And what we do in the United States is make it easy to gamble with other people's money—particularly borrowed money—by making sure that almost everybody who makes bad loans gets their money back anyway. The financial crisis of 2008 was a natural result of these perverse incentives.

# 1

# Gambling with Other People's Money

Imagine a superb poker player who asks you for a loan to finance his nightly poker playing.[1] For every $100 he gambles, he's willing to put up $3 of his own money. He wants you to lend him the rest. You will not get a stake in his winning. Instead, he'll give you a fixed rate of interest on your $97 loan.

The poker player likes this situation for two reasons. First, it minimizes his downside risk. He can only lose $3. Second, borrowing has a great effect on his investment—it gets leveraged. If his $100 bet ends up yielding $103, he has made a lot more than 3 percent—in fact, he has doubled his money. His $3 investment is now worth $6.

But why would you, the lender, play this game? It's a pretty risky game for you. Suppose your friend starts out with a stake of $10,000 for the night, putting up $300 himself and borrowing $9,700 from you. If he loses anything more than 3 percent on the night, he can't make good on your loan.

Not to worry—your friend is an extremely skilled and prudent poker player who knows when to hold 'em and when to fold 'em. He may lose a hand or two because poker is a game of chance, but by the end of the night, he's always ahead. He always makes good on his debts to you. He has never had a losing evening. As a creditor of the poker player, this is all you care about. As long as he can make good on his debt, you're fine. You only care about one thing—that he stays solvent so that he can repay his loan and you get your money back.

But the gambler cares about two things. Sure, he too wants to stay solvent. Insolvency wipes out his investment, which is always unpleasant—it's bad for his reputation and hurts his chances of being able to use leverage in the future. But the gambler doesn't just care about avoiding the downside. He also cares about the upside. You as the lender don't share in the upside—no matter how much money the gambler makes on his bets, you just get your promised amount of interest.

If there is a chance to win a lot of money, the gambler is willing to take a big risk. After all, *his* downside is small. He only has $3 at stake. To gain a really large pot of money, the gambler will take a chance on an inside straight.

As the lender of the bulk of his funds, you wouldn't want the gambler to take that chance. You know that when the leverage ratio, the ratio of borrowed funds to personal assets, is 32–1, the gambler will take a lot more risk than you'd like. So you keep an eye on the gambler to make sure that he continues to be successful in his play.

But suppose the gambler becomes increasingly reckless. He begins to draw to an inside straight from time to time and pursue other high-risk strategies that require making very large bets that threaten his ability to make good on his promises to you. After all, it's worth it to him.

He's not playing with very much of his own money. He is playing mostly with your money. How will you respond?

You might stop lending altogether, concerned that you will lose both your interest and your principal. Or you might look for ways to protect yourself. You might demand a higher rate of interest. You might ask the player to put up his own assets as collateral in case he is wiped out. You might impose a covenant that legally restricts the gambler's behavior, barring him from drawing to an inside straight, for example.

These would be the natural responses of lenders and creditors when a borrower takes on increasing amounts of risk. But this poker game isn't proceeding in a natural state. There's another person in the room: Uncle Sam. Uncle Sam is off in the corner, keeping an eye on the game, making comments from time to time, and every once in a while, intervening in the game. He sets many of the rules that govern the play of the game. And sometimes he makes good on the debt of the players who borrow and go bust, taking care of the lenders. After all, Uncle Sam is loaded. He has access to funds that no one else has. He also likes to earn the affection of people by giving them money. Everyone in the room knows Uncle Sam is loaded, and everyone in the room knows there is a chance, perhaps a very good chance, that wealthy Uncle Sam will cover the debts of players who go broke.

Nothing is certain. But the greater the chance that Uncle Sam will cover the debts of the poker player if he goes bust, the less likely you are to try to restrain your friend's behavior at the table. Uncle Sam's interference has changed your incentive to respond when your friend makes riskier and riskier bets.

GAMBLING WITH OTHER PEOPLE'S MONEY

If you think that Uncle Sam will cover your friend's debts . . .

- you will worry less and pay less attention to the risk-taking behavior of your gambler friend.
- you will not take steps to restrain reckless risk-taking.
- you will keep making loans even as his bets get riskier.
- you will require a relatively low rate of interest for your loans.
- you will continue to lend even as your gambler friend becomes more leveraged.
- you will not require that your friend put in more of his own money and less of yours as he makes riskier and riskier bets.

What will your friend do when you behave this way? He'll take more risks than he would normally. Why wouldn't he? He doesn't have much skin in the game in the first place. You do, but your incentive to protect your money goes down when you have Uncle Sam as a potential backstop.

Capitalism is a profit *and* loss system. The profits encourage risk-taking. The losses encourage prudence. Eliminate losses or even raise the chance that there will be no losses and you get less prudence. So when public decisions reduce losses, it isn't surprising that people are more reckless.

Who got to play with other people's money? Who was highly leveraged—putting very little of their own money at risk while borrowing the rest? Who was able to continue to borrow at low rates even as they made riskier and riskier bets? Who sat at the poker table?

Just about everybody.

Homebuyers. The government-sponsored enterprises (GSEs)—Fannie Mae and Freddie Mac. The commercial banks—Bank of America, Citibank, and many others. The investment banks—like Bear Stearns and Lehman Brothers. Everyone was playing the same game, playing with other people's money. They were all able to continue borrowing at the same low rates even as the bets they placed grew riskier and riskier. Only at the very end, when collapse was imminent and there was doubt about whether Uncle Sam would really come to the rescue, did the players at the table find it hard to borrow and gamble with other people's money.

Without extreme leverage, the housing meltdown would have been like the meltdown in high-tech stocks in 2001—a bad set of events in one corner of a very large and diversified economy.[2] Firms that invested in that corner would have had a bad quarter or a bad year. But because of the amount of leverage that was used, the firms that invested in housing—Fannie Mae and Freddie Mac, Bear Stearns, Lehman Brothers, Merrill Lynch, and others—destroyed themselves.

So why did it happen? Did bondholders and lenders really believe that they would be rescued if their investments turned out to be worthless? Were the expectations of a bailout sufficiently high to reduce the constraints on leverage? And even though it is pleasant to gamble with other people's money, wasn't a lot of that money really their own? Even if bondholders and lenders didn't restrain the recklessness of those to whom they lent, why didn't stockholders—who were completely wiped out in almost every case, losing their entire investments—restrain recklessness? Sure, bondholders and lenders care only about avoiding the downside. But stockholders don't care just about the upside. They don't want to be wiped out, either. The executives of Fannie Mae, Freddie Mac, and the large investment banks held millions, sometimes hundreds of millions, of their own wealth in equity in their firms. They didn't want to go broke and lose all that money. Shouldn't that have restrained the riskiness of the bets that these firms took?

# 2

# Did Creditors Expect to Get Rescued?

Was it reasonable for either investors or their creditors to expect government rescue?[1] While there were government bailouts of Lockheed and Chrysler in the 1970s, the recent history of rescuing large, troubled financial institutions began in 1984, when Continental Illinois, then one of the top ten banks in the United States, was rescued before it could fail. The story of its collapse sounds all too familiar—investments that Continental Illinois had made with borrowed money turned out to be riskier than the market had anticipated. This caused what was effectively a run on the bank, and Continental Illinois found itself unable to cover its debts with new loans.

In the government rescue, the government took on $4.5 billion of bad loans and received an 80 percent equity share in the bank. Only 10 percent of the bank's deposits were insured, but every depositor was covered in the rescue.[2] Eventually, equity holders were wiped out.

In congressional testimony after the rescue, the Comptroller of the Currency implied that there were no attractive alternatives to such rescues if the 10 or 11 largest banks in the United States experienced similar problems.[3] The rescue of Continental Illinois and the subsequent congressional testimony sent a signal to the poker players and those that lend to them that lenders might be rescued.

Continental Illinois was just the largest and most dramatic example of a bank failure where creditors were spared any pain. Irvine Sprague, in his 1986 book *Bailout*, noted, "Of the fifty largest bank failures in history, forty-six—including the top twenty—were handled either through a pure bailout or an FDIC assisted transaction where no depositor or creditor, insured or uninsured, lost a penny."[4]

The 50 largest failures up to that time all took place in the 1970s and 1980s. As the savings and loan (S&L) crisis unfolded during the 1980s, government repeatedly sent the same message: lenders and creditors would get all their money back. Between 1979 and 1989, 1,100 commercial banks failed. Out of all of their deposits, 99.7 percent, insured or uninsured, were reimbursed by policy decisions.[5]

The next event that provided information to the poker players was the collapse of Drexel Burnham in 1990.[6] Drexel Burnham lobbied the government for a guarantee of its bad assets that would allow a suitor to find the company attractive. But Drexel went bankrupt with no direct help from the government. The failure to rescue Drexel put some threat of loss back into the system, but maybe not very much—Drexel Burnham was a political pariah. The firm and its employees had numerous convictions for securities fraud and other violations.

In 1995, there was another rescue, not of a financial institution, but of a country—Mexico. The United

States orchestrated a $50 billion rescue of the Mexican government, but as in the case of Continental Illinois, it was really a rescue of the creditors, those who had bought Mexican bonds and who faced large losses if Mexico were to default. As Charles Parker details in his 2005 study, Wall Street investment banks had strong interests in Mexico's financial health (because of future underwriting fees) and held a significant number of Mexican bonds and securities.[7] Despite opposition from Main Street and numerous politicians, policy makers put together the rescue in the name of avoiding a financial crisis. Ultimately, the US Treasury got its money back and even made a modest profit, causing some to deem the rescue a success. It was a success in fiscal terms. But it encouraged lenders to finance risky bets without fear of the consequences.

Willem Buiter, then an economics professor at the University of Cambridge, now the chief economist at CitiGroup, was quoted at the time saying,

> This is not a great incentive for efficient operations of financial markets, because people do not have to weigh carefully risk against return. They're given a one-way bet, with the U.S. Treasury and the international community underwriting the default risk. That makes for lazy private investors who don't have to do their homework figuring out what the risks are.[8]

Or to put it a little more informally, all profit and no loss make Jack a dull boy.

The next major relevant event on Wall Street was the 1998 collapse of Long-Term Capital Management (LTCM), a highly leveraged private hedge fund.[9] When its investments soured, its access to liquidity dried up and it faced insolvency. There was a fear that the death of LTCM would take down many of its creditors.

The president of the Federal Reserve Bank of New York, William McDonough, convened a meeting of the major creditors—Bankers Trust, Barclays, Bear Stearns, Chase Manhattan, Credit Suisse, First Boston, Deutsche Bank, Goldman Sachs, J. P. Morgan, Lehman Brothers, Merrill Lynch, Morgan Stanley, Parabas, Solomon Smith Barney, Société Générale, and UBS. The meeting was "voluntary," as was ultimately the participation in the rescue that the Fed orchestrated.

Most of the creditors agreed to put up $300 million apiece. Lehman Brothers put up $100 million. Bear Stearns contributed nothing. Altogether, they raised $3.625 billion. In return, the creditors received 90 percent of the firm. Ultimately, LTCM died. While creditors were damaged, the losses were much smaller than they would have been in a bankruptcy. No government money was involved. Yet the rescue of LTCM did send a signal that the government would try to prevent bankruptcy and creditor losses.

In addition to all of these public and dramatic interventions by the Fed and the Treasury, there were many examples of regulatory forbearance—where government regulators suspended compliance with capital requirements. There were also the seemingly systematic efforts by the Federal Reserve beginning in 1987 and continuing throughout the Greenspan and Bernanke eras to use

monetary policy to keep asset prices (equities and housing, in particular) bubbling along.[10] All of these actions
reduced investors' and creditors' worries of losses.[11]

That brings us to the current mess that began in
March 2008. There is seemingly little rhyme or reason
to the pattern of government intervention. The government played matchmaker and helped Bear Stearns get
married to J. P. Morgan Chase. The government essentially nationalized Fannie and Freddie, placed them into
conservatorship, and is honoring their debts and funding
their ongoing operations through the Federal Reserve.
The government bought a large stake in AIG and hon-
ored all of its obligations at 100 cents on the dollar. The
government funneled money to many commercial banks.

Each case seems different. But there is a pattern. Each
time, the stockholders in these firms were either wiped
out or saw their investments reduced to a trivial fraction
of what they were before. The bondholders and lenders were left untouched. In every case other than that of
Lehman Brothers and Washington Mutual, bondholders
and lenders received everything they were promised:
100 cents on the dollar. Many of the poker players—and
almost all of those who financed the poker players—lived
to fight another day. It's the same story as Continental
Illinois, Mexico, and LTCM—a complete rescue of creditors and lenders.

The most important and much-discussed exception
to the rescue pattern was Lehman. Its creditors had to
go through the uncertainty, delay, and the likely losses
of bankruptcy. The balance sheet at Lehman looked a
lot like the balance sheet at Bear Stearns—lots of subprime securities and lots of leverage. What should

executives at Lehman have done in the wake of Bear Stearns's collapse? What would you do if you were part of the executive team at Lehman and you had seen your storied competitor disappear? The death of Bear Stearns should have been a wake-up call. But the rescue of Bear's creditors let Lehman keep playing the same game as before.

If Bear had been left to die, there would have been pressure on Lehman to raise capital, get rid of the junk on its balance sheet, and clean up its act. There were a variety of problems with this strategy: Lehman might have found it hard to raise capital. It might have found that the junk on its balance sheet was worth very little, and it might not have been worth it for the company to clean up its act. What Lehman actually did, though, is unclear. It appears to have raised some extra cash and sold off some assets. But it remained highly leveraged, still at least 25–1 in the summer of 2008.[12] How did it keep borrowing at all given the collapse of Bear Stearns?

One of Lehman's lenders was the Reserve Primary money market fund. It held $785 million of Lehman Brothers commercial paper when Lehman collapsed. When Lehman entered bankruptcy, those holdings were deemed to be worthless, and Reserve Primary broke the buck, lowering its net asset value to 97 cents. Money market funds are considered extremely safe investments in that their net asset value normally remains constant at $1, but on that day, Reserve Primary's fund holders suffered a capital loss. What was a money market fund doing investing in Lehman Brothers debt in the aftermath of the Bear Stearns debacle? Didn't Reserve's executives know Lehman's balance sheet looked a lot like Bear's? Surely they did. Presumably they assumed that the government would treat Lehman like Bear. It seems they expected a rescue in the worst-case scenario.

They weren't alone. When Bear collapsed, Lehman's credit default swaps spiked, but then fell steadily after Bear's creditors were rescued, through mid-May (figure 1), even as the price of Lehman's stock fell steadily after January.[13] This suggests that investors expected Lehman to be rescued, as Bear was, in the case of a Lehman collapse.[14] Many economists have blamed the government's failure to rescue Lehman as the cause of the panic that ensued.[15] But why would Lehman's failure cause a panic? What was the new information that investors reacted to? After the failure of Bear Stearns, many speculated that Lehman was next. It was well known that Lehman's balance sheet was highly leveraged with assets similar to Bear's.[16] The government's refusal to rescue Lehman, or at least its creditors, caused the financial market to shudder, not because of any direct consequences of a Lehman bankruptcy but because it signaled that the implicit policy of rescuing creditors might not continue.

The new information in the Lehman collapse was that future creditors might indeed be at risk and that the party might be over. That conclusion was quickly reversed with the rescue of AIG and others. But it sure sobered up the drinkers for a while.

Did this history of government rescuing creditors and lenders encourage the recklessness of the lenders who financed the bad bets that led to the financial crisis of 2008?

Figure 1. The Annual Cost to Buy Protection against Default on $10 Million of Lehman Debt for Five Years

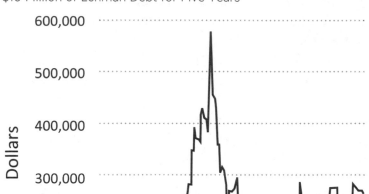

Months of 2008

*Source:* Phoenix Partners Group.

For the GSEs' creditors, the answer is almost certainly yes. Fannie Mae and Freddie Mac's counterparties expected the US government to stand behind Fannie and Freddie, which of course it ultimately did. This belief allowed Fannie and Freddie to borrow at rates near those of the Treasury.

From January 2000 through mid-2003, the spreads of Fannie Mae and Freddie Mac bonds vs. Treasuries—the rate at which Fannie and Freddie could borrow money compared to the US government—were low and falling. Those spreads stayed low and steady through early 2007. Between 2000 and fall 2008 when Fannie and Freddie were essentially nationalized, the rate on Fannie and Freddie's five-year debt over and above Treasuries was almost always less than 1 percent. From 2003 through 2006, it was about a third of a percentage point.[17] Yet between 2000 and 2007, as I show below, Fannie and Freddie were acquiring riskier and riskier loans, which ultimately led to their death. Why didn't lenders to Fannie and Freddie require a bigger premium as Fannie and Freddie took on more risk?

The answer is that they saw lending to the GSEs as no riskier than lending money to the US government. Not quite the same, of course. GSEs do not have quite the same credit risk as the US government. There was a chance that the government would let Fannie or Freddie go bankrupt. That's why the premium rose in 2007, but even then, it was still under 1 percent through September 2008.[18]

The unprecedented expansion of Fannie and Freddie's activities even as their portfolio became riskier helped create the housing bubble. This eventually led to their demise and conservatorship, the polite name for what is really nationalization. The government has already paid out over $100 billion on Fannie and Freddie's behalf, with a much higher bill likely to come in the future.[19]

But what about the lenders to the commercial banks and the investment banks? Yes, the government bailed out all the lenders other than those that lent to Lehman and Washington Mutual. Yes, many institutions that had made bad bets survived instead of going bankrupt. But did this reality and all the rescues of the 1980s and 1990s really affect the behavior of lenders in advance of the rescues?

We can't know with certainty. No banker will step forward and say that past bailouts and the "Greenspan put" caused him to be less prudent and made him feel good about lending money to Bear Stearns. No executive at Bear Stearns will say that he reassured nervous lenders by telling them that the government would step in. And Goldman Sachs continues to claim that it is part of a "virtuous cycle" of raising capital and creating wealth and jobs, that it converted into a bank holding company to "restore confidence in the financial system as a whole," and that the rescue of AIG had no effect on its bottom line.[20] (Right. And I'm going to be the starting point guard for the Boston Celtics next year.)

While direct evidence is unlikely, the indirect evidence relies on how people generally behave in situations of uncertainty. When expected costs are lowered, people behave more recklessly. When football players make a tackle, they don't consciously think about the helmet protecting them, but safer football equipment encourages more violence on the field. Few people think that it's okay to drive faster on a rainy night when they have seatbelts, airbags, and antilock brakes, but that is how they behave.[21] Not all motivations are direct and conscious.[22]

There is even some evidence of conscious expectations of rescue, though it is necessarily anecdotal. Andrew Haldane, the executive director of Financial Stability of the Bank of England, tells this story about stress-testing, simulations that banks conduct to examine worst-case scenarios for interest rates, the state of the economy, and so on, to make sure they have enough capital to survive:

> A few years ago, ahead of the present crisis, the Bank of England and the FSA [Financial Services Authority] commenced a series of seminars with financial firms, exploring their stress-testing practices. The first meeting of that group sticks in my mind. We had asked firms to tell us the sorts of stress which they routinely used for their stress-tests. A quick survey suggested these were very modest stresses. We asked why. Perhaps disaster myopia—disappointing, but perhaps unsurprising? Or network externalities—we understood how difficult these were to capture?
>
> No. There was a much simpler explanation according to one of those present. There was absolutely no incentive for individuals or teams to run severe stress tests and show these to management. First, because if there were such a severe shock, they would very likely lose their bonus and possibly their jobs. Second, because in that event the authorities would have to step-in anyway to save a bank and others suffering a similar plight.
>
> All of the other assembled bankers began subjecting their shoes to intense scrutiny. The unspoken words had been spoken. The officials in the room were aghast. Did banks not understand that the official sector would not underwrite banks mismanaging their risks?
>
> Yet history now tells us that the unnamed banker was spot-on. His was a brilliant articula-

tion of the internal and external incentive problem within banks. When the big one came, his bonus went and the government duly rode to the rescue.[23]

The only difference between this scenario in the United Kingdom and the one in the United States is that, in the United States, the Fed came to the rescue, *and* the executives, for the most part, kept their bonuses.

3

# What about Equity Holders?

C reditors do not share in the upside of any investment. So they only care about one thing—avoiding the downside. They want to make sure their counterparty is going to stay solvent. Equity holders care about two things—the upside and the downside. So why doesn't fear of the downside encourage prudence? Even if creditors were lulled into complacency by the prospects of rescue, shareholders— who are usually wiped out—wouldn't want too much risk, would they?

Why would Bear Stearns, Lehman Brothers, and Merrill Lynch take on so much risk? They didn't want to go bankrupt and wipe out the equity holders. Why would these firms leverage themselves 30–1 and 40–1, putting the existence of the firm at risk in the event of a small change in the value of the assets in their portfolios? Surely the equity holders would rebel against such leverage.

But very few equity holders put all their eggs in one basket. Buying risky stocks isn't just for highfliers looking for high risk and high rewards. It also attracts people who want high risk and high rewards in *part* of their portfolios. It's all about risk and return along with diversification. The Fannie Mae stock held in an investor's portfolio might be high risk and (she hopes) high return. If that makes a Fannie Mae stockholder nervous, she can also buy Fannie Mae bonds. The bonds are low risk, low return. She can even hold a mix of equity and bonds to mimic the overall return to Fannie Mae in its entirety. For every $100 she invests, she buys $98 of Fannie's bonds and $2 of equity. When the stock is doing well, the equity share boosts the return of the safe bonds. In the worst-case scenario, Fannie Mae goes broke, wiping out the investor's equity. But in the meantime, she made money on the bonds and maybe even on the stocks, if she got out in time.

The same is true of investors holding Bear Stearns or Lehman stock. In 2005, Bear Stearns had its own online subprime mortgage lender, BearDirect. Bear Stearns also owned EMC, a subprime mortgage company. Bear was generating subprime loans and bundling them into mortgage-backed securities, making an enormous amount of money as the price of housing continued to rise. All through 2006 and most of 2007, things weren't just fine. They were better than fine. The price of Bear Stearns's stock hit $172. If an investor sold then or even a lot later, she did very, very well. Even though she knew there was a risk that the stock could not just go down, but go down a lot, she didn't want to discourage the risk-taking. She wanted to profit from it.

# 4

# Heads—They Win a Ridiculously Enormous Amount; Tails—They Win Just an Enormous Amount

But what about the executives of Bear Stearns, Lehman Brothers, or Merrill Lynch? Their investments were much less diversified than those of the equity holders. Year after year, the executives were being paid in cash and stock options until their equity holdings in their own firms became a massive part of their wealth. Wouldn't that encourage prudence?

Let's go back to the poker table and consider how the incentives work when the poker player isn't just risking his own money alongside that of his lenders. He's also drawing a salary and bonus and stock options while he's playing. Some of that compensation is a function of the profitability of the company, which appears to align the incentives of the executives with those of other equity holders. But when leverage is so large, the executive can take riskier bets, generating large profits in the short run and justifying a larger salary. The downside risk is cushioned by his ability to accumulate salary and bonuses in advance of failure.

As Lucian Bebchuk and Holger Spamann have shown, the incentives in the banking business are such that the expected returns to bank executives from bad investments can be quite large even when the effects on the firm are quite harmful. The upside is unlimited for the executives while the downside is truncated:

> Because top bank executives were paid with shares of a bank holding company or options on such shares, and both banks and bank holding companies obtained capital from debt-holders, executives faced asymmetric payoffs, expecting to benefit more from large gains than to lose from large losses of a similar magnitude. . . .
>
> Our basic argument can be seen in a simple example. A bank has $100 of assets financed by $90 of deposits and $10 of capital, of which $4 are debt and $6 are equity; the bank's equity is in turn held by a bank holding company, which is financed by $2 of debt and $4 of equity and has no other assets; and the bank manager is compensated with some shares in the bank holding company. On the downside, limited liability protects the manager from the consequences of any losses beyond $4. By contrast, the benefits to the manager from gains on the upside are unlimited. If the manager does not own stock in the holding company but rather options on its stock, the incentives are even more skewed. For example, if the exercise price of the option is equal to the current stock price, and the manager makes a negative-expected-value bet, the manager may have a great deal to gain if the bet turns out well and little to lose if the bet turns out poorly.[1]

George Akerlof and Paul Romer describe similar incentives in the context of the S&L collapse.[2] In "Looting: The Economic Underworld of Bankruptcy for Profit," they describe how the owners of savings and loans would book accounting profits, justifying a large salary even though those profits had little or no chance of becoming real. They would generate cash flow by offering an attractive rate on the savings accounts they offered. Depositors would not worry about the viability of the banks because of Federal Deposit Insurance Corporation (FDIC) insurance. But the owners' salaries were ultimately coming out of the pockets of taxpayers. What the owners were doing was borrowing money to finance their salaries, money that the taxpayers guaranteed. When the S&Ls failed, the depositors got their money back, and the owners had their salaries: the taxpayers were the only losers.

This kind of looting and corruption of incentives is only possible when you can borrow to finance highly leveraged positions. This in turn is only possible if lenders and bondholders are fools—or if they are very smart and are willing to finance highly leveraged bets because they anticipate government rescue.

In the current crisis, commercial banks, investment banks, and Fannie and Freddie generated large short-term profits using extreme leverage. These short-term profits alongside rapid growth justified enormous salaries until the collapse came. Who lost when this game collapsed? In almost all cases, the lenders who financed the growth avoided the costs. The taxpayers got stuck with the bill, just as they did in the S&L crisis. Ultimately, the gamblers were playing with other people's money and not their own.

But didn't executives lose a great deal of money when their companies collapsed? Why didn't fear of that outcome deter excessive risk-taking on their parts? After all, Jimmy Cayne, the CEO of Bear Stearns, and Richard Fuld, the CEO of Lehman Brothers, each lost over a billion dollars when their stock holdings were virtually wiped out. Jimmy Cayne ended up selling his six million shares of Bear Stearns for just over $10 per share. Fuld ended up selling millions of shares for pennies per share. Surely they didn't want this to happen.

They certainly didn't *intend* for it to happen. This was a game of risk and reward, and in this round, the cards didn't come through. That was a gamble the executives had been willing to take in light of the huge rewards they had already earned and the even larger rewards they would have pocketed if the gamble had gone well. They saw it as a risk well worth taking.

After all, their personal downsides weren't anything close to zero. Here is Cayne's assessment of the outcome: "The only people [who] are going to suffer are my heirs, not me. Because when you have a billion six and you lose a billion, you're not exactly like crippled, right?"[3]

The worst that could happen to Cayne in the collapse of Bear Stearns, his downside risk, was a stock wipeout, which would leave him with a mere half a billion dollars gained from his prudent selling of shares of Bear Stearns and the judicious investment of the cash part of his compensation.[4] Not surprisingly, Cayne didn't put all his eggs in one basket. He left himself a healthy nest egg outside of Bear Stearns.

Fuld did the same thing. He lost a billion dollars of paper wealth, but he retained over $500 million, the value of the Lehman stock he sold between 2003 and 2008. Like Cayne, he surely would have preferred to be worth $1.5 billion instead of a mere half a billion, but his downside risk was still small.

When we look at Cayne and Fuld, it is easy to focus on the lost billions and overlook the hundreds of millions they kept. It is also easy to forget that the outcome was not preordained. They didn't plan on destroying their firms. They didn't intend to. They took a chance. Maybe housing prices plateau instead of plummet. Then you get your $1.5 billion. It was a roll of the dice. They lost.

When Cayne and Fuld were playing with other people's money, they doubled down, the ultimate gamblers. When they were playing with their own money, they were prudent. They acted like bankers. (Or the way bankers once acted when their own money or the money of their partnership was at stake.)[5] They held a significant number of personal funds outside of their own companies' stock, making their downside risks much smaller than they appeared. They each had a big cushion to land on when their companies went over the cliff. Those cushions were made from other people's money, the money that was borrowed, the money that let them make high rates of return while the good times rolled and justified their big compensation packages until things fell apart.

What about the executives of other companies? Cayne and Fuld weren't alone. Angelo Mozilo, the CEO of Countrywide, realized over $400 million in compensation between 2003 and 2008.[6] Numerous executives made over $100 million in compensation during the same period.[7] Lucian Bebchuk, Alma

Cohen, and Holger Spamann have looked at the sum of cash bonuses and stock sales by the CEOs and the next four executives at Bear Stearns and Lehman Brothers between 2000 and 2008. It's a very depressing spectacle. The top five Bear Stearns executives managed to score $1.5 billion during that period. The top five executives at Lehman Brothers had to settle for $1 billion.[8] Nice work if you can get it.

The standard explanations for the meltdown on Wall Street are that executives were overconfident. Or they believed their models that assumed Gaussian distributions of risk when the distributions actually had fat tails. Or they believed the ratings agencies. Or they believed that housing prices couldn't fall. Or they believed some permutation of these many explanations.

These explanations all have some truth in them. But the undeniable fact is that these allegedly myopic and overconfident people didn't endure any economic hardship because of their decisions. The executives never paid the price. Market forces didn't punish them, because the expectation of future rescue inhibited market forces. The "loser" lenders became fabulously rich by having enormous amounts of leverage, leverage often provided by another lender, implicitly backed with taxpayer money that did in fact ultimately take care of the lenders.

And many gamblers won. Lloyd Blankfein, the CEO of Goldman Sachs, Jamie Dimon, the CEO of J. P. Morgan Chase, and the others played the same game as Cayne and Fuld. Goldman and J. P. Morgan invested in subprime mortgages. They were highly leveraged. They didn't have as much toxic waste on their balance sheets as some of their competitors. They didn't have quite as much leverage, but they were still close to the edge. They were playing a very high-stakes game, with high-risk and potential reward. And they survived. Blankfein's stock in Goldman Sachs is worth over $500 million, and like Cayne and Fuld, he surely has a few assets elsewhere. Like Cayne and Fuld, Blankfein took tremendous risk with the prospect of high reward. His high monetary reward came through, as did his intangible reward in the perpetual poker game of ego. Unlike Cayne and Fuld, Blankfein and Dimon get to hold their heads extra high at the cocktail parties, political fundraisers, and charity events, not just because they're still worth an immense amount of money, but because they won. They beat the house.

But does creditor rescue explain too much? If it's true that bank executives had an incentive to finance risky bets using leverage, why didn't they take advantage of the implicit guarantee even sooner, investing in riskier assets and using ever more leverage? Banks and investment banks didn't take wild risks on Internet stocks leading to bankruptcy and destruction. Why didn't commercial banks and investment banks take on more risk sooner?

One answer is that when the guarantee is implicit, not explicit, creditors can't finance any investment regardless of how risky it is. If a bank lends money to another bank to buy stock in an Australian gold-mining company, it is less likely to get bailed out than if the money goes toward AAA-rated assets (which are the highest quality and lowest risk). So some high-risk gambles remain unattractive. That is part of the answer. But the rest of the answer is due to the nature of regulation. In the next section, I look at why housing and securitized mortgages were so attractive to investors financing risky bets with borrowed money. Bad regulation and an expectation of creditor rescue worked together to destroy the housing market.

# 5

# How Creditor Rescue and Housing Policy Combined with Regulation to Blow Up the Housing Market

The proximate cause of the housing market's collapse was the same proximate cause of the financial market's destruction—too much leverage, too much borrowed money. Just as a highly leveraged investment bank risks insolvency if the value of its assets declines by a small amount, so too does a homeowner.

The buyer of a house who puts 3 percent down and borrows the rest is like the poker player. Being able to buy a house with only 3 percent down, or ideally even less, is a wonderful opportunity for the buyer to make a highly leveraged investment. With little skin in the game, the buyer is willing to take on a lot more risk when buying a house than if she had to put up 20 percent. And for many potential homebuyers, a low down payment is the only way to sit at the table at all.

When prices are rising, buying a house with little or no money down seems like a pretty good deal. Let's say the house is in California, and the price of the house is $200,000. For $6,000 (3 percent down), the buyer has a stake in an asset that has been appreciating in some markets in some years at 20 percent. If this trend continues, a year from now, the house will be worth $40,000 more than she paid for it. The buyer will have seen a more than six-fold increase in her investment.

What is the downside risk? The downside risk is that housing prices level off or go down. If housing prices do go down a lot, the buyer could lose her $6,000, and she may also lose her house or find herself making monthly payments on an asset that is declining in value and therefore a very bad investment. This is why many homebuyers are currently defaulting on their mortgages and forfeiting any equity they once had in the house. In some states, in the case of default, the lender could go after her other assets as well, but in a lot of states—including California and Arizona, for example—the loan is what is called "non-recourse"—the lender can foreclose on the house and get whatever the house is worth but nothing else. Failing to pay the mortgage and losing your house is embarrassing and inconvenient, and, if you have a good credit rating, it will hurt even more. But the appeal of this deal to many buyers is clear, particularly when housing prices have been rising year after year after year.

The opportunity to borrow money with a 3 percent down payment has three effects on the housing market:

- It allows people who normally wouldn't have accumulated a sufficient down payment to buy a house.

- It encourages a homeowner to bid on a larger, more expensive house rather than a cheaper one.

- For a house of any particular value, it encourages the buyer to bid more than the house is currently worth if there is expected appreciation.[1]

These circumstances all push up the demand for housing. And, of course, if housing prices ever fall, these loans will very quickly be underwater (meaning that the homeowner will owe more on the home than it is currently worth). A small decrease in housing values will cause a homeowner who put 3 percent down to have negative equity much quicker than a buyer who put 20 percent down. With a zero-down loan, the effects are even stronger. But in the early 2000s, a low down payment loan was like a lottery ticket with an unusually good chance of paying off. A zero-down loan was even better. And some loans not only didn't require a down payment, but also covered closing costs.

Changes in tax policy sweetened the deal. The Taxpayer Relief Act of 1997 made the first $250,000 ($500,000 for married couples) of capital gains from the sale of a primary residence tax exempt.[2] Sellers no longer had to roll the profits over into a new purchase of equal or greater value. The act even allowed the capital gains on a second home, a pure investment, to be tax-free as long as you lived in that house for two of the previous five years. This tax policy change increased the value of the lottery ticket.

The cost of the lottery ticket depended on interest rates. In 2001, worried about deflation and recession and the stock market, Alan Greenspan lowered the federal funds rate (the rate at which banks can borrow money from each other) to its lowest level in forty years and kept it there for about three years.[3] During this time, the rate on fixed-rate mortgages was falling, but the rate on adjustable rate mortgages, a short-term

Figure 2. S&P/Case-Shiller House Price Indices,
1991–2009 (1991 Q1=100)

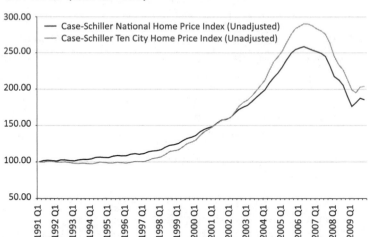

*Source:* Author's calculations based on data presented in Scott Frame, Andreas Lehnert, and Ned Prescott, "A Snapshot of Mortgage Conditions with an Emphasis on Subprime Mortgage Performance," paper presented to the Federal Reserve's Home Mortgage Initiatives Coordinating Committee, April 27, 2008, http://federalreserveonline.org/pdf/MF_Knowledge_Snapshot-082708.pdf.

interest rate, fell even more, widening the gap between the two. Adjustable rate mortgages grew in popularity as a result.[4]

The falling interest rates, particularly on adjustable rate mortgages, meant that the price of the lottery ticket was falling dramatically. And as housing prices continued to rise, the probability of winning appeared to be going up (see figure 2). The upside potential was large. The downside risk was very small—mainly the monthly mortgage payment, which was offset by the advantage of being able to live in the house. Who wouldn't want to invest in an asset that has a likely tax-free capital gain, that the buyer can enjoy in the meantime by living in it, and that she can own without using any of her own money? By 2005, 43 percent of first-time buyers were putting no money down, and 68 percent were putting down less than 10 percent.[5]

Incredibly, the buyer could even control how much the ticket cost. In a 2006 speech, Fannie Mae CEO Daniel Mudd outlined how monthly loan payments could differ when buying a $425,000 house, the average value of a house in the Washington, DC, area at the time:

- With a standard fixed-rate mortgage, the monthly payment is about $2,150.

- With a standard adjustable rate mortgage, the payment drops $65, down to about $2,100 a month.

- With an interest-only adjustable rate mortgage, the monthly payment drops nearly another $300, down to $1,795.

- With an option adjustable rate mortgage, the payment could drop another $540, down to roughly $1,250—which in many cases, is less than one would pay to rent a two-bedroom apartment. Of course, that's only in the first year.[6]

In 2005, the average house in the Washington, DC, area grew in value by about 24 percent.[7] For the average house bought for $425,000, that's a gain of more than $100,000. The annual payment of that option adjustable rate mortgage was $15,000. That's a pretty cheap lottery ticket for a chance to win $100,000 if prices rise in 2006 by the same amount as the year before. The buyer is paying less than she would in rent, and on top of that, she has a chance to win $100,000. Why wouldn't a person with limited wealth want to get into that game? Why wouldn't a person with lots of wealth?

Figure 3. Issuance of Mortgage-Backed Securities, 1985–2009 (in billions of dollars)

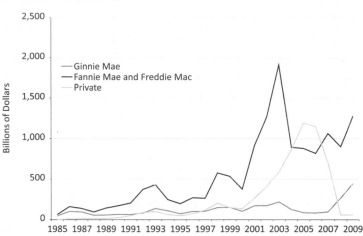

*Source:* Author's calculations based on data from *Inside Mortgage Finance.*

It's obvious why buyers liked buying houses with little or no money down and the impact that opportunity had on the price of housing, but why would anyone lend money to buyers who had so little money of their own in a transaction? It's the same question we asked earlier at the poker table. Why would anyone finance risky bets knowing that the bettor has so little skin in the game?

There are two reasons you might lend a lot of money to someone with no money of their own in the transaction. If home prices are rising and have been for a while, you might be pretty confident that they'll continue to rise. In that case, the borrower will have equity in the home at the end of the year, and the chance of default will be smaller than it would normally be. You might take a chance and lend the money. But it's a chance.

This is one explanation for the explosive growth of mortgage securitization—no one thought housing prices would go down (see figure 3). That could be. Yet, historically, nobody made loans where the borrower put little or no money down.

The second reason is that you will be very comfortable lending the money if you know you can sell the loan to someone else. Who is that someone? Between 1998 and 2003, the most frequent buyers of loans were the government-sponsored enterprises Fannie Mae and Freddie Mac.

Fannie and Freddie bought those loans with borrowed money. Fannie and Freddie were able to borrow the money because the lenders were confident that Uncle Sam stood behind Fannie and Freddie.

# 6

# Fannie and Freddie

*The goal of this strategy, to boost homeownership to 67.5 percent by the year 2000, would take us to an all-time high, helping as many as 8 million American families across that threshold. . . . I want to say this one more time, and I want to thank again all the people here from the private sector who have worked with Secretary Cisneros on this: Our homeownership strategy will not cost the taxpayers one extra cent.[1]*
—President Bill Clinton

*We want more people owning their own home. It is in our national interest that more people own their own home. After all, if you own your own home, you have a vital stake in the future of our country.[2]*
—President George W. Bush

T he federal government's role in the housing market goes back at least to 1938 with the establishment of the Federal National Mortgage Association (which later became Fannie Mae) and the deductibility of mortgage interest, which is as old as the income tax.[3] But the federal government's role changed fundamentally in the 1990s, when it (along with state governments) pursued a wide array of policies to increase the national homeownership rate. I focus here on the most important change—the expansion of the role of Fannie Mae and Freddie Mac, particularly their expansion into low down payment loans.[4]

Some, such as Paul Krugman, argue that Fannie and Freddie had nothing to do with the housing crisis. They were not allowed to make low down payment loans; they were not allowed to make subprime loans. They were simply innocent bystanders caught in the crossfire.[5] Krugman has also argued a number of times that Fannie and Freddie's role in housing markets was insignificant between 2004 and 2006: "they pulled back sharply after 2003, just when housing really got crazy." According to Krugman, Fannie and Freddie "largely faded from the scene during the height of the housing bubble."

In fact, from 2000 on, Fannie and Freddie bought loans with low FICO scores, loans with very low down payments, and loans with little or no documentation—Alt-A loans.[6] And between 2004 and 2006, Fannie and Freddie didn't "fade away" or "pull back sharply." As I show below, they still bought near-record numbers of mortgages, including an ever-growing number of low down payment mortgages. And while private players bought many more subprime loans than the GSEs, the GSEs purchased hundreds of billions of dollars of subprime mortgage-backed securities (MBS) from private issuers, holding these securities as investments:

Fannie and Freddie bought 25.2% of the record $272.81 billion in subprime MBS sold in the first half of 2006, according to *Inside Mortgage Finance Publications,* a Bethesda, MD–based publisher that covers the home loan industry.

In 2005, Fannie and Freddie purchased 35.3% of all subprime MBS, the publication estimated. The year before, the two purchased almost 44% of all subprime MBS sold.[7]

The defenders of Fannie and Freddie are right that Fannie and Freddie's direct role in subprime lending was smaller than that of purely private financial institutions. But between 1998 and 2003, Fannie and Freddie played an important role in pushing up the demand for housing at the low end of the market. That in turn made subprime loans increasingly attractive to other financial institutions.

## IT'S ALIVE!

The word "conduit" is often used to describe Fannie and Freddie's role in the mortgage market. A conduit is a tube or pipe. Just as a tube or a pipe carries water to raise the level of a reservoir, so Fannie and Freddie added liquidity to the mortgage market, increasing the level of the funds available so that more could partake. That additional liquidity steered by Fannie and Freddie to increase loan availability above and beyond what it would be otherwise seems to be a free lunch of sorts—a way to overcome the natural impediments of timing and risk facing banks and thrifts at very little cost.

Fannie and Freddie increased liquidity to the mortgage market by buying loans from mortgage originators. Banks were happy to sell their loans and give up some of the profit because this meant they wouldn't have to worry about lending money today that wouldn't return for years, with all the risks of default, interest rate changes, and prepayment. Fannie and Freddie financed their purchases of loans by issuing debt. They also bundled the mortgages into securities, selling those to investors. Eventually, Fannie and Freddie also used their profits to buy the mortgage-backed securities and collateralized debt obligations issued by other players in the market.

Fannie and Freddie did indeed make homeownership more affordable and accessible. Joseph Stiglitz, in his book *The Roaring Nineties*, argued that the original incarnation of Fannie (as an actual government agency before it was semiprivatized in 1968) was a classic example of fixing a market failure:

> Fannie Mae, the Federal National Mortgage Association, was created in 1938 to provide mortgages to average Americans, because private mortgage markets were not doing their job. Fannie Mae has resulted both in lower mortgage rates and higher home-ownership—which has broader social consequences. Homeowners are more likely to take better care of their houses and also to be more active in the community in which they live.[8]

But Fannie and Freddie (created in 1970) were not the textbook creations of economists. At some point,

Fannie and Freddie stopped acting like models in a textbook and became something more than conduits. Politicians realized that steering Fannie and Freddie's activities produced political benefits. And Fannie and Freddie found it profitable to be steered.

Fannie and Freddie had always had certain cost advantages that were not available to purely private players in the mortgage business. They were not subject to the same Securities and Exchange Commission disclosure regulations when they issued mortgage-backed securities. They were not subject to state and local income taxes. Both Fannie and Freddie could tap a credit line of $2.25 billion with the Treasury. The amount of capital they were required to hold was much smaller than that required of private firms.

But the most important advantage for Fannie and Freddie was the implicit government guarantee, embodied in the first letter of their names, the letter "F" for Federal. Fannie Mae's original name was the Federal National Mortgage Association. Freddie Mac was the Federal Home Loan Mortgage Corporation. Investors believed correctly that the federal government stood behind Fannie and Freddie, which were, after all, called GSEs: government-sponsored enterprises. At the same time, Fannie and Freddie were publicly traded corporations with stockholders.

The business model at Fannie and Freddie was very simple. Because of the government guarantee, they could borrow money cheaply. They could then earn money by buying mortgages that paid a higher rate of interest than the rate Fannie and Freddie had to pay to their lenders. It was a money machine that was

Figure 4. Combined Earnings of Fannie and Freddie, 1971–2007 (in billions of 2009 dollars)

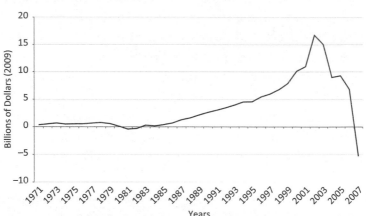

*Source:* Author's calculations based on data from 2008 OFHEO Report to Congress (author's conversion to 2009 dollars).

incredibly profitable (see figure 4).[9] There was only one constraint—the government didn't let Fannie and Freddie exploit this opportunity fully.

Because the government might be on the hook for any losses, Fannie and Freddie operated under a regulatory regime where they could only buy what were called "conforming loans"—loans with at least 20 percent down, loans no bigger than a certain amount, and loans with adequate documentation. These restrictions limited Fannie and Freddie's ability to expand and take advantage of the implicit guarantees from the government. There are only so many borrowers who can put 20 percent down.

But beginning in 1993, these restraints began to loosen.[10] Fannie and Freddie faced new regulations requiring minimum proportions of their loan purchases to be loans made to borrowers with incomes below the median. In 1993, 30 percent of Freddie's and 34 percent of Fannie's purchased loans were loans made to individuals with incomes below the median in their area. The new regulations required that number to be at least 40 percent in 1996.[11] The requirement rose to 42 percent in 1999 and continued to rise through the 2000s, reaching 55 percent in 2007.[12] Fannie and Freddie hit these rising goals every year between 1996 and 2007.[13]

These requirements seemed like such a good idea at the time. Why not spread the benefits of homeownership more widely? Why not take advantage of the spread between the interest rate at which Fannie and Freddie could borrow and lend? Why not increase Fannie and Freddie's profits? It seemed like such a magical free lunch: more homeowners, more profits, and more politicians who could claim they were helping people.

Which brings us to one other group sitting at the table playing with other people's money: politicians. Politicians are always eager to spend other people's money. It's what they do for a living. But it's an even better deal for politicians if they can hide the fact that they're spending other people's money or delay when the bill comes due. That's what they hid with Fannie and Freddie. The politicians told Fannie and Freddie to be a little more flexible with their guidelines. As a result, more people got to own houses and the politicians got to take the credit without having to raise taxes or take away any politically provided goodies from anyone else.

Fannie and Freddie's increases in loan purchases, especially loans to low-income borrowers, helped inflate the housing bubble. That bubble in turn made

Figure 5. Home Purchase Loans Bought by GSEs, 1996–2007

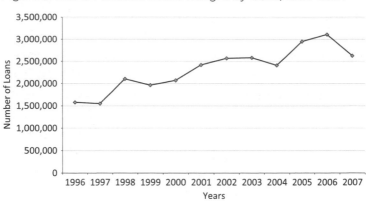

*Source:* Author's calculations based on data from HUD, "Profiles of GSE Mortgage Purchases," Tables 10a and 10b, http://www.huduser.org/portal/datasets/gse/profiles.html. Data from 1998 received from FHFA via personal correspondence. Tables 10a and 10b received from FHFA in personal correspondence.

the subprime market more attractive and profitable to lenders. It also set the stage for the collapse. Housing policy interacting with the potential for creditor rescue pushed up housing prices artificially. When it all fell apart, the taxpayer paid (and is still paying) the bill.

In the crucial years of housing-price appreciation, between 1997 and 2006, the number of loans bought by Fannie and Freddie expanded dramatically. Figure 5 shows the number of home purchase loans bought by Fannie and Freddie. Home purchase loans are loans used by borrowers to purchase homes (rather than to refinance homes). The number jumped by roughly 33 percent in 1998, then by another 25 percent in 2001, and by another 20 percent in 2005. The annual number of loans they purchased doubled between 1997 and 2006.

As figure 6 shows, Fannie and Freddie's purchases of home purchase loans made to borrowers with incomes

Figure 6. Total Home Purchase Loans Bought by GSEs for
Below-Median-Income Buyers, 1996–2007

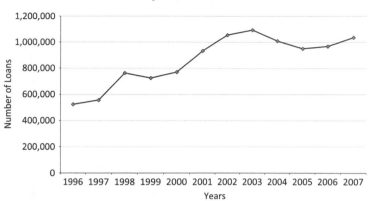

*Source:* Author's calculations based on data from HUD, "Profiles of GSE Mortgage Purchases," Tables 10a
and 10b, http://www.huduser.org/portal/datasets/gse/profiles.html. Data from 1998 received from FHFA
via personal correspondence. Tables 10a and 10b received from FHFA in personal correspondence.

below the median grew even more quickly. These purchases more than doubled.

Fannie and Freddie's purchases of low down payment loans (loans with a down payment of 5 percent or
less, or a 95 percent loan-to-value ratio) increased at an
even faster rate (see figure 7).

But if Fannie and Freddie could only buy conforming loans—with at least 20 percent down, loans no bigger than a certain amount, and loans with adequate
documentation—how did the opportunities available
to Fannie and Freddie expand so incredibly? With
the encouragement of politicians from both parties,
Fannie and Freddie relaxed their underwriting standards, the requirements they placed on originators
before they would buy a loan. They called it being more
"flexible."[14]

Figure 7. Total Home Purchase Loans Bought by
GSEs with Greater than 95% Loan-to-Value Ratio, 1998–2007

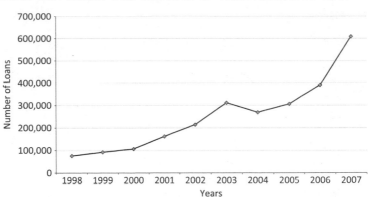

*Source:* Author's calculations based on data from HUD, "Profiles of GSE Mortgage Purchases," Tables 10a and 10b, http://www.huduser.org/portal/datasets/gse/profiles.html. Data from 1998 received from FHFA via personal correspondence. Tables 10a and 10b received from FHFA in personal correspondence.

For loans made to low-income borrowers, they created special partnerships, using new criteria to determine whether they would buy a loan from an originator.[15] They partnered with some of those originators, the traditional lenders—local and national banks—to develop new products with more "flexible" standards and terms.[16] And they got fancy with technology.

Around 1995, both Fannie and Freddie unveiled automated software for originating loans: Desktop Underwriter and Loan Prospector, respectively. The software made assessing the riskiness of loans more "scientific" by using credit scores. Fannie and Freddie claimed that based on statistical analyses of the relationship between credit scores and default rates, loans that were once considered too risky were now actually fine.[17] These software programs allowed Fannie and Freddie to do an end run around the traditional lenders, creating a cottage industry of mortgage brokers who originated loans for Fannie and Freddie. The software made it cheaper to originate a loan. That was a good thing. But it also allowed more "flexibility" in lending standards, which ended up being a very bad thing.

A *Christian Science Monitor* article from 2000 discussed the impact of automated underwriting:

So for borrowers with good credit, the automated system allows higher debt-to-income ratios than conventional underwriting. That means a borrower might qualify for a larger loan than someone with the same income and poorer credit.

Some other advantages of automated underwriting:

- It requires less documentation. "Where three months of bank statements and paycheck stubs are required for conventional underwriting, only one month is typically required by the automated system," says Ms. James.
- Borrowers are being approved for loans that they would have been turned down for just a year or two ago.

"By analyzing the credit assessments done by Desktop Underwriter, we found that lower-income families have credit histories that are just as strong as wealthier families," said Fannie Mae chief executive Frank Raines in a speech to the National Association of Home Builders. As a result, 44 percent of Fannie Mae's business is now conducted with low- and moderate-income families. Mr. Raines added that having a strong credit history could offset the need for a large down payment.[18]

The most important change at Fannie and Freddie, however, was their approach to the down payment. In 1997, fewer than 3 percent of Fannie and Freddie's loans had a down payment of less than 5 percent.[19] But starting in 1998, Fannie created explicit programs where the required down payment was only 3 percent. In 2001, they even began purchasing loans with zero down. With loans that had a down payment, they stopped requiring the borrower to come up with the down payment out of her own funds. Down payments could be gifts from friends or, better still, grants from a nonprofit or government agency.

These changes weren't secret; executives and politicians bragged about how Fannie and Freddie were buying riskier loans. Frank Raines, the CEO of Fannie Mae at the time, testified before the US House Committee of Financial Services in 2002:

> For example, a down payment is often the single largest obstacle preventing a family from purchasing a home. Fannie Mae was at the forefront of the mortgage industry expansion into low-down payment lending and created the first standardized 3-percent-down mortgage. Fannie Mae financing for low down payment loans (5 percent or less) has grown from $109 million in 1993 to $17 billion in 2002.
>
> We've also used technology to expand our underwriting criteria, so that we can reach under-

served communities. For example, our Expanded Approval products make it possible for people with blemished credit to obtain a conforming mortgage loan. And we've added a Timely Payments Reward feature to those loans, enabling borrowers to lower their mortgage payment by making their payments on time. These mortgage features have been crucial tools in reaching into communities that were previously underserved. The mortgage market today has a wider variety of products available than ever before, and therefore is better poised to meet the individual financing needs of a broader range of homebuyers.[20]

Between 1998 and 2003, the absolute number of loans purchased by Fannie and Freddie with less than 5 percent down more than quadrupled (see table 1). Also by 2003, 714,000 loans, 28 percent of Fannie and Freddie's total volume of home purchase loans, were loans with less than 10 percent down.[21]

When the down payment was less than 20 percent, Fannie and Freddie required private mortgage insurance (PMI). On a zero-down payment loan, for example, the borrower would take out insurance to cover 20 percent of the value of the loan, protecting Fannie and Freddie from the risk of the borrower defaulting. But starting in the 1990s, an alternative to PMI emerged—the piggyback loan, a second loan that finances part or all of the entire down payment. The use of piggyback loans grew quickly beginning in the 1990s through 2003 and even more dramatically in the 2004–2006 period.[22] For example, in a study of the Massachusetts mortgage

Table 1. Owner-Occupied Home Loans with Less than
5 Percent Down Purchased by Fannie and Freddie per Year,
1998–2007

| Year | Number of loans | % of Fannie and Freddie owner-occupied home purchase loans w/less than 5 percent down |
|---|---|---|
| 1998 | 75,694 | 4 |
| 1999 | 91,938 | 5 |
| 2000 | 106,398 | 5 |
| 2001 | 162,369 | 7 |
| 2002 | 214,424 | 8 |
| 2003 | 311,285 | 12 |
| 2004 | 268,731 | 11 |
| 2005 | 306,128 | 12 |
| 2006 | 390,000 | 15 |
| 2007 | 608,581 | 23 |

*Source:* Author's calculations based on data from HUD, "Profiles of GSE Mortgage Purchases," Tables 10a and 10b, http://www.huduser.org/portal/datasets/gse/profiles.html. Data from 1998 received from FHFA via personal correspondence. Tables 10a and 10b received from FHFA in personal correspondence.

market, the Warren Group found that in 1995, piggy-back loans were 5 percent of prime mortgages. The number grew to 15 percent by 2003. By 2006, over 30 percent of prime mortgages in Massachusetts were financed with piggyback loans. For subprime loans in Massachusetts, almost 30 percent were financed with piggybacks in 2003 and more than 60 percent by 2006.[23]

There are no public data yet available on how many of Fannie's loans with 20 percent down were really piggyback loans with zero down—loans where the borrower had no equity in the house. Suffice it to say that Fannie and Freddie contributed to the zero or low down payment frenzy with their support of 3 percent down and eventually no money down loans. The full extent of Fannie and Freddie's involvement in low down payment loans is unclear because of the piggyback phenomenon. Maybe we'll find out down the road.

## WHAT STEERING THE CONDUIT REALLY DID

Whether one measures by the total number of loans or by dollar volume, Fannie and Freddie took the originate-and-sell model of mortgage lending through the roof. What was really going on? Individuals, institutions, and governments were lending money to Fannie and Freddie, who used that money to buy loans from originators, who gave that money to people, who used that money to buy homes. Fannie and Freddie were conduits for investors to make loans to homeowners. Fannie and Freddie did so in wildly increasing amounts even as the quality of the loans deteriorated. Perhaps they did it in blind exuberance. But they were encouraged to be blind. When the government implicitly backed Fannie and Freddie, it severed the usual feedback loops of a market system.

The fees that Fannie and Freddie paid their originators made origination extremely profitable. Because there was no feedback loop that punished bad loans, many more bad loans were made. Not only did people borrow money as a lottery ticket, but surely originators encouraged potential homeowners by deceiving them about the financial products they were buying.[24] The implicit guarantee of Fannie and Freddie and the housing mandates removed the normal restraints of prudence on homeowners and originators.

Consider an investing odd couple: the Chinese government on the one hand and my father, a cautious investor in his 70s, on the other. Both invested in Fannie and Freddie bonds because they paid more interest than Treasuries and were probably just as safe. They weren't paying attention to what was going on with Fannie and Freddie's portfolio of loans because they didn't need to. They counted on the implicit guarantee. It was a free lunch for my father and the Chinese—a good return without any risk. We know investors weren't paying attention because between 2000 and 2006, even as Fannie and Freddie took on more and more risk, Fannie and Freddie's borrowing costs stayed constant or even fell relative to Treasuries. The market viewed bonds issued by Fannie and Freddie as almost interchangeable with Treasuries. Alas, the market was right.[25]

The American taxpayer ultimately paid for that "free lunch." And a few trillion dollars flowed from the Chinese and my father and other investors into new houses and bigger houses because the Fannie and Freddie conduit offered such an attractive mix of risk and reward. That flow of money was terribly costly: channeling precious capital into housing meant it didn't flow into other areas that were more valuable but that were artificially made less attractive. So we got more and bigger houses and less of something else—less money going to fund new medical devices, or cars that get better gas mileage, or more creative entertainment, or something else creative people could have done with more capital.

# 7

# Fannie and Freddie—
# Cause or Effect?

P eople inside the mortgage and investment world have two different perspectives on Fannie and Freddie's role. The first view is that Fannie and Freddie were followers, not leaders. They put up with the affordable housing mandates because they were already involved in loans to low-income borrowers. They loosened credit standards between 1998 and 2003 to keep market share. They got involved in Alt-A and subprime loans in 2005 and 2006 for the same reason. They were just victims of the crisis.[1]

The second view is best summarized by a hedge fund manager who told me that Fannie and Freddie "made their own weather." Fannie and Freddie were such a large part of the market's liquidity that they were the underlying cause of what went wrong. They created the originate-and-sell market. They steered the mortgage lending business with the dominance of their automated underwriting systems. Encouraged by HUD, they poured hundreds of billions of dollars into home purchases made by borrowers with low incomes. And ultimately, through their purchases of subprime securities (purchases they used to help satisfy their

HUD affordable housing goals),[2] they helped create the market for subprime.[3]

There is some truth in both views. It's important to distinguish between two periods: the mid-1990s through the early 2000s, when subprime was relatively unimportant, and 2000 onward—especially 2004 onward—when subprime grew dramatically. Before 2004, Fannie and Freddie definitely helped inflate the bubble. The question is by how much? Did they make a large difference, or did their growth merely crowd out Federal Housing Administration (FHA) and private mortgage activity?[4] Did their substantial purchases of private label mortgage-backed securities expand the demand, or would other investors simply have made those purchases?

These are hard questions to answer in any systematic way. Fannie and Freddie activity in one city may have no effect on housing prices because of supply conditions in that market. Elsewhere, pushing up the demand may have dramatic effects. Controlling for all of the relevant factors is extremely difficult. The same is true for estimating Fannie and Freddie's impact on the demand for subprime mortgage-backed securities.

There is strong evidence that the availability of mortgage credit had much to do with the pre-2004 period in which prices were rising and homeownership reached record heights.[5] Long before the surge in subprime securitization, lenders were making a lot more loans to people who normally wouldn't have received loans. Some of this lending was based on irrational exuberance.

But much of it came from a national policy pushed by a Democratic and then a Republican administration to encourage homeownership.

Initially cautious about meeting those housing goals, Fannie and Freddie became more aggressive. They played a significant part in the expansion of mortgage credit to low-income borrowers, an expansion that presumably pushed up housing prices in low-income neighborhoods, making subprime securitization more attractive.

My judgment is that Fannie and Freddie helped push up the price of housing and inflate the housing bubble between 1998 and 2003, though it may be hard to know the magnitude of their impact with any precision. But this isn't the whole story of the rise in housing prices during this period. The availability of piggyback loans and federal and state programs to help people buy houses with no money down did much to create home-owners with little or no home equity, the proximate cause of the crisis.[6]

After 2003, Fannie and Freddie didn't exactly stand on the sidelines. They didn't "fade away" or "pull back sharply." Between 2004 and 2006, they still purchased almost a million home loans each year made to borrowers with incomes below the median. They still purchased 268,000 loans with less than 5 percent down in 2004, almost 400,000 such loans in 2006, and over 600,000 such loans in 2007. They purchased hundreds of billions of subprime mortgage-backed securities and were a significant part of the demand for those securities.

What is true is that between 2004 and 2006, commercial banks and investment banks were bigger direct players than the GSEs in the subprime market. The role of commercial banks and investment banks in the subprime market is the rest of the story.

# 8

# Commercial Banks and Investment Banks

Countrywide, Bank of America, Bear Stearns, Lehman Brothers, Merrill Lynch, and the others weren't government-sponsored enterprises. They were private firms, commercial and investment banks, that originated subprime mortgages and issued private label mortgage-backed securities. But what the banks and Wall Street were doing was very similar to what Fannie and Freddie were doing—they were borrowing at a relatively low rate and lending at a relatively higher one. If you can manage that, you make money on the spread.

Why could they borrow at such low rates? There were two reasons—they borrowed very short term (sometimes overnight). They also had the implicit guarantee that Fannie and Freddie had, though it was certainly less certain for the investment banks than for Fannie and Freddie. The other difference between the government-sponsored enterprises and Wall Street firms is that Fannie and Freddie were borrowing from people outside the poker game—the Chinese government, individual investors, insurance companies. But in the case of the investment banks, their lenders were often the other gamblers around the table. Lehman Brothers, Merrill Lynch, Bank of America, and Credit Suisse were all major investors in subprime securities. Some were more invested than others. Some were more leveraged than others. But they were all financing others' seats at the table.

When the price of houses grows by at least 10 percent annually for almost a decade, you can imagine making a loan to someone with a lousy credit history and no money down—a borrower who puts no money down can have substantial equity in the house, greatly reducing the risk of default.

The rising prices of houses created the opportunity for subprime securitization and the financing of riskier mortgages generally. According to *Inside Mortgage Finance*, the subprime market grew steadily from $100 billion in 2000 to over $600 billion in 2006. Alt-A mortgages went from being insignificant in 2000 to $400 billion in 2006. So by 2006, there was a trillion dollars' worth of high-risk mortgages (see figure 8).

In 2006, Alt-A and subprime mortgages were one-third of all originations. Some of those risky loans were bought and held or securitized by Fannie and Freddie. But most of those mortgages were bought and held by large financial institutions that had nothing to do with a government housing mandate or US housing policy. US housing policy helped to inflate the housing bubble that made a high-risk loan imaginable. But what were these private investors thinking? Why were they pouring money into risky loans?

Figure 8. Value of Mortgage Originations, 1990–2008
(in billions of dollars)

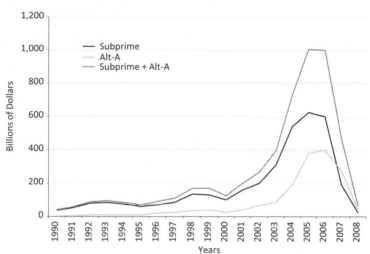

*Source:* Author's calculations based on data from *Inside Mortgage Finance*.

A lot of people made a lot of money making these loans before the market collapsed in 2007 and 2008. The lenders made money by selling the loans to the GSEs and to Wall Street firms or by holding onto them. The borrowers made money as their houses appreciated and they sold, enjoyed the equity, or took that equity out via a home equity line of credit. The people who bought the securities packaged by the GSEs and Wall Street did well. As long as the prices kept rising, everything was better than fine. And some people got out in time. They sold their houses. They sold their mortgage-backed securities before the default rates rose.

But too many people kept dancing like crazy even when the music began to slow down and then came to a halt. Why did so many people invest so much money in what turned out to be incredibly risky assets?

One answer is that they believed in the risk assessment models that said that mortgage-backed securities and collateralized debt obligations (CDOs) were very safe, even when the mortgages were subprime. The AAA-rated portions were supposed to be as safe as Treasuries. The logic of the tranching system was the logic of the *Titanic*—damage would be contained and absorbed by the lower tranches. The AAA tranches were unsinkable. That was how risky assets could be turned into AAA assets. But like the *Titanic*, there is always an iceberg big enough to break enough compartments so that the damage cannot be contained.

For those who accept this narrative, the subprime collapse is a lesson in hubris, greed, and myopia—irrational exuberance run wild. The investment bankers believed their risk models that said that the AAA portions of mortgage-backed securities were safer than safe—and that the risk of bankruptcy was therefore very small.[1] This failure of imagination, this failure to appreciate the real odds of a housing collapse, explains part of the enthusiasm investors had for an asset that was appreciating year after year.

One problem with this explanation is that many practitioners were surely aware of the shortcomings of their models. Consider Riccardo Rebonato, the chief risk officer of the Royal Bank of Scotland (RBS). In his thoughtful book *The Plight of the Fortune Tellers*, written before the crisis, he argued that the standard measures of risk, such as Value at Risk (VaR), were not as reliable as they seemed and that the whole enterprise of risk management is less scientific than it appears.[2] I presume that Rebonato knew that RBS was on thin ice as it expanded its purchases of mortgage-backed securities. Shortly after Rebonato's book was published, the Bank of England took over RBS because of the collapse in the value of RBS's investments. I suspect Rebonato warned his bosses plenty about the risks they were taking. They either viewed the situation differently or their incentives reduced the appeal of prudence.

Another problem with the irrational exuberance explanation is that it wasn't really the same asset appreciating year after year. The fundamentals of the asset were steadily deteriorating. The proportion of the mortgage market that was subprime was increasing. The investors were lending money to finance increasingly risky loans. And yet the money kept flowing. Why? Was it simply human frailty or were the natural incentives for restraint distorted by public policy?

In the first part of this book, I argued that an expectation of creditor bailout encouraged lenders to finance much riskier investments than borrowers would have financed had they had more of their own skin in the game. But there is a puzzle. The large financial institutions that were highly leveraged invested mostly in the safest assets, not the riskiest ones. They purchased the most senior tranches of mortgage-backed securities. True, these did not turn out to be as safe as they appeared. But there were much riskier mortgage-backed products—the junior tranches for example—or much riskier assets not related to housing. Why did financial institutions pour money into housing, particularly the safest parts of housing, given my earlier story about the poker game? Why didn't the investment banks invest in even riskier assets given that they were playing with other people's money?

# 9
# Picking Up Nickels

L et's return to the metaphor of the poker table. As a player sitting at the table drawing a salary based on your performance and able to enhance the measure of your performance by leveraging the money of your investors with borrowed money, what is the ideal investment?

A high-risk, high-return investment has drawbacks. If you draw to an inside straight with borrowed money, you will sometimes win a very big pot. But most of the time, you'll lose and be unable to pay off your loans. Then you'll lose your seat at the table, be unable to draw a salary, and have a harder time getting a seat in the future. And if creditors believe that their ability to be repaid depends on the reasonableness of the investments to which they lent money, a player who keeps drawing to an inside straight may have trouble attracting funds.

A much better approach is to look for investments that have a small risk of failure (even though the consequences of failure are catastrophic) and a small return. No one loves a small return, but leverage improves the overall return of such a portfolio. That was part of the appeal of mortgage-backed securities.[1]

On Wall Street, the practice of making small amounts of money on a lot of transactions while knowing that eventually the whole thing can fall apart and you might get flattened is called "picking up nickels in front of a steamroller." Picking up nickels in front of a steamroller is a very appealing game.[2] True, the steamroller might get you. Your firm might die. But you live to earn another day (especially if everyone else was doing the same thing). And while you're picking up the nickels, you look like a genius. Year after year you make excellent rates of return justifying a very large salary and bonus. The ideal bet for the poker player playing with other people's money and drawing a salary isn't just a risky bet. It's a risky bet with a low chance of disaster and high chance of a modest return.

Long-Term Capital Management's strategy was picking up nickels—making very small amounts on arbitrage opportunities with very high leverage. The steamroller did get them in 1998. But they made a lot of money along the way for their executives and for their creditors who got rescued or at least partially rescued—and that was just *one* firm picking up nickels. When everyone is picking up nickels in front of the steamroller, the odds of a complete rescue are higher. So when a bunch of firms got flattened, Uncle Sam came to the rescue, using taxpayer money to cover the hospital bills.

As in the Fannie and Freddie story, the real financers of the salaries associated with picking up the nickels aren't the firms. The taxpayers are ultimately funding the picking up of the nickels, and the taxpayers get flattened. The executives at the firms that manage to pick up just the right number of nickels and stay ahead of the steamroller (Goldman and J. P. Morgan) make ridiculously enormous amounts of compensation. The executives at the firms that get steamrolled (Bear Stearns, Lehman, Citibank, etc.) just make an enormous amount of money. The real risks are borne by you and me.

# 10
# Basel—Faulty

T he other part of the appeal of mortgage-backed securities came from a change in regulation. American and European regulators began requiring compliance with many of the features of Basel II, the name for the regulatory changes that were expected around 2008 but adopted in practice before that date.[1]

Beginning in 2002, for example, commercial banks were allowed to leverage AAA- and AA-rated securities 60–1.[2] A-rated securities could be leveraged 25–1, BBB 12–1, and BB 8–1. A 60–1 leverage ratio means investing $1.60 of your own money for every $100 you invest. You borrow the rest. Of course, that means that if those securities lost value, a mere 2 percent reduction in the value of the asset would not cover what you owed, and you risked insolvency or bankruptcy.

These changes seemed reasonable from the outside. They required banks to hold more capital for riskier investments but less capital for the safest classes—AAA and AA. I can find no contemporaneous press coverage of these changes. It seems no one was paying any attention in the media, and rightfully so: capital requirements are boring. But I suspect the commercial banks and investment banks were paying a great deal of attention as these regulations were discussed and negotiated in the Basel process.

These changes created a demand for AAA- and AA-rated opportunities. For the commercial banks and the investment banks, such opportunities were like conforming loans were to Fannie and Freddie: highly profitable, but limited in number. But the investment community found a way to get around the restraint. The tranching system of CDOs was a way to create AAA-rated investments out of loans that were highly risky. This financial alchemy was particularly attractive because of the regulatory change.[3]

Many observers have blamed the ratings agencies for significantly contributing to the crisis because they gave AAA ratings to the tranches of mortgage-backed securities that were created out of toxic assets and that eventually poisoned even the senior tranches. Much is made of the fact that the issuers of these securities paid for the ratings, which compromised the integrity of the agencies.

The problem with these explanations is that most investors knew that the issuers were paying the agencies. They also knew that these assets were extremely complex and that the agencies may have lacked the expertise needed to analyze the assets correctly. They took the ratings with many grains of salt. The commercial banks bought the assets, not because they trusted the agencies, but because they could leverage them under the new regulations. The investment banks bought the assets because they were highly profitable and easy to borrow against.

The lower capital requirements for AAA- and AA-rated securities helped fuel the demand for subprime mortgage-backed securities and helped create the crisis. But just because your car can go 120 miles per hour doesn't mean you'll choose to go that fast. Why would a firm want to take advantage of this deregulation and put itself at risk of bankruptcy? And how would a firm be able to take advantage of this looser capital requirement? Why would anyone lend them the money?

Lenders lent the money because they could expect to be rescued, and for the most part they were. Firms borrowed the money because borrowing gave the executives in the firm glorious individual payoffs. The AAA-rated super senior tranches did not pay particularly well even while the music was playing. As one hedge fund manager told me, "I could never understand why there was such a demand for the senior tranches—the return was lousy." But with enough leverage, say 60–1, they looked a lot better. A hedge fund couldn't play that game; an investment bank could.

At one level, this story is just a natural response to incentives. Because AAA-rated investments were "safer," there was an incentive to create them. There was an incentive to figure out a way to price them. There was an incentive to figure out a way to expand them (using subprime loans and lots of alchemy), and there was an incentive to expand them further (synthetic CDOs). But none of these incentives make sense without leverage, and the leverage makes no sense without the prospect of creditor rescue.

The most plausible alternative explanation is some variation on irrational exuberance, coupled perhaps with rational exuberance—players trying to profit from the rise in housing prices even while knowing it may not last. But as I have shown, the key players weren't reckless with their own money. They made sure to invest it elsewhere. When it was their own money, they picked up quarters rather than nickels in markets that were relatively free from steamrollers. And they made sure that regulations that might have restrained their ability to exploit the system (looser capital requirements) were relaxed, so they could effectively use taxpayer money instead of their own to fund the risky investments.

Could Wall Street have gotten into this game even without implicit guarantees to creditors? The creditors did say no to Bear Stearns eventually—to its hedge fund in 2007 and to the firm as a whole in 2008. Was that because they worried that the government wouldn't come to their rescue? After all, the borrowing and lending were very short term, suggesting a wariness of the future. Or was the short-term nature of the borrowing just an additional way to hold down costs? Yet it does so in a risky way. Given the systematic rescue of creditors in recent decades, it is hard to believe that the strong possibility of rescue did not play a role in the increasing amounts of leverage and risk.

# 11

# Where Do We Go from Here?

An unpleasant but unavoidable conclusion is that Wall Street was (and remains) a giant government-sanctioned Ponzi scheme. Homebuyers borrowed money from lenders who got their money from Fannie Mae, Freddie Mac, and banks that borrowed money from investors who expected to be reimbursed by the politicians who took that money from taxpayers. Almost everyone made money from this deal except the group left holding the bag—the taxpayers. There is an old saying in poker: If you don't know who the sucker is at the table, it's probably you. We are the suckers. And most of us didn't even know we were sitting at the table.

Many people have placed the current mess at the doorstep of capitalism. But Milton Friedman liked to point out that capitalism is a profit and loss system.[1] The profits encourage risk-taking. The losses encourage prudence. Government policies have made too many markets one-sided. Because of implicit government guarantees, the gains were private and the losses were public. The policies allowed people to gamble with other people's money, and by rescuing the creditors of Fannie

Mae, Freddie Mac, Bear Stearns, AIG, Merrill Lynch, and others, policy makers have further weakened the natural restraints of the profit and loss system. This isn't capitalism—it is crony capitalism.

Even those who are skeptical of the role of creditor rescue in creating this crisis understand that it has raised the chance of the next one. The standard policy response is to reduce the size of financial institutions to make them small enough to be able to fail, restrict executive pay to reduce the potential for looting, and increase capital requirements to reduce the fragility of the system induced by leverage.

But the symbiotic dance between politicians and Wall Street is why so many proposed reforms are unlikely to be successful for very long.[2] Fannie and Freddie had their own regulator. We've had capital requirements. Yet these attempts at oversight failed. The firms and the executives with the biggest stake in the outcomes made sure that the system served them rather than the taxpayer.

Part of the reason reform is so difficult is that the interaction between politicians, regulators, and investors is a complex system that we don't fully understand. F. A. Hayek understood the challenges of engineering a complex system from the top down when he wrote, "The curious task of economics is to demonstrate to men how little they really know about what they imagine they can design." Economists and regulators imagine we can design a better financial system. Hayek would argue that such efforts are inherently flawed. That's why the next time is never different.

Instead of trying to improve a system we only imperfectly understand, we would have better luck letting the natural restraints of capitalism reemerge. Rather than trying to turn this dial or push that lever the optimal amount (holding everything else constant, somehow), we should let natural feedback loops reemerge that encourage prudence as well as risk-taking.

Here are some changes that would move us away from crony capitalism and toward the real thing:

- Don't try to re-create the old system while trying to make it "better." There is a natural wariness about securitization right now. That is good. Let it blossom. There is a natural wariness about zero-down mortgages. That is good. Let it blossom.

- Recognize that having every American own a home is not the American Dream, but the dream of the National Association of Home Builders and the National Association of Realtors. The government should fund any government programs to increase homeownership out of current tax dollars where the costs are visible. Don't reform Fannie and Freddie. Don't resurrect them. Get the government out of the business of hidden subsidies to mortgage interest rates.

- Be aware that the Fed is certainly part of the problem and may not be part of the solution. The Fed created the artificially low interest rates that helped inflate the housing bubble. The Fed then raised interest rates too quickly, with disastrous effects for the adjustable rate mortgages encouraged by their low interest rate policy. Monetary policy should not be left to any self-proclaimed or publicly anointed maestro. Following an automatic money growth rule or the Taylor rule would have avoided much of the pain. Somebody needs to hold the Fed accountable for funding exuberance.

- Restrain rather than empower the Fed. It has played a major role in exacerbating the moral hazard problem. It is not good for a democracy to have an agency as unaccountable as the Fed acquire even more power and use it in ad hoc ways.

- Take the "crony" out of "crony capitalism." Rescues have distorted the natural feedback loops of capitalism. Removing the cronies will not be easy, and economists should not make it more difficult. The near universal praise by economists for the actions of Bernanke, Paulson, and Geithner and the near universal condemnation by economists of the decision to let Lehman Brothers enter bankruptcy greatly reduce the credibility of any promise by policy makers to act differently in the future.

- Stop enabling obscene transfers of wealth. In this crisis, average Americans have sent hundreds of billions of dollars to some of the richest people in human history. This has been done over and over again in the name of avoiding a crisis, akin to putting out every forest fire. But this only postpones the day of reckoning. Eventually a conflagration comes along that consumes everything. The better the citizenry understands this reality, the better the chance that political incentives will change. If people don't understand it, the political incentives will stay in place. Economists play an important role in how people perceive what has happened. We should stop being the enablers of such obscene transfers of wealth by claiming they are necessary for stability.

- Excoriate, condemn, and call to account rather than praise and honor policy makers who make creditors and lenders whole. Zero cents on the dollar for bankrupt bets made by lenders and creditors would be ideal, but it is unlikely to be a credible promise. So let's start more modestly. A ceiling of 50 cents on the dollar for creditors and lenders when the institutions they fund become insolvent is a natural place to start. Even this may be too difficult for politicians to stomach. But economists should be able to support such a move and preach its virtues.

Rescuing rich people from the consequences of their decisions with money coming from average Americans is bad for democracy. It is bad for democracy because the Fed and the Treasury are spending trillions of dollars of taxpayer money with very little accountability or transparency. It's bad for democracy because it means that some people have to live with the consequences of their decisions while others get rescued. That in turn creates a very destructive feedback loop of rent-seeking, where losers seek government help after the fact rather than make careful decisions before the fact.

Rescuing people from the consequences of their decisions is bad for capitalism. It means that a distorted calculus of risk and reward allocates trillions of dollars of capital. The biggest mistake of the last decade of distorted incentives is that trillions of dollars poured into more and bigger houses instead of into better medical devices or new forms of entertainment or more efficient cars. It was a bad deal private decision makers would never have made on their own. It was a bad deal that only took place because public policy distorted the incentives.

Is it really imaginable that we can regain a profit and loss system, a true capitalism where people take responsibility for their actions instead of relying on being bailed out by those more prudent than themselves? It's up to us. All we have to do is demand politicians who feel the same way. We need to look in the mirror. Too many of us applauded when Presidents Clinton and Bush pushed for higher and higher homeownership rates. Too many of us applauded when Fannie and Freddie were asked to "give something back" and become more "flexible." Too many of us applauded when Wall Street was rescued. If we as voters more fully understood the consequences of those decisions, we might get different politicians and policy makers, or at least politicians and policy makers who will make different decisions the next time around.

Milton Friedman once observed that people mistakenly believe that electing the right people is the key to better public policy. "It's nice to elect the right people," he said, "but that isn't the way you solve things. The way you solve things is to make it politically profitable for the wrong people to do the right things."[3] To do that, we, the people, have to favor a different philosophy for the relationship between Washington and Wall Street than the one we have now. We have to favor a relationship where there is both profit and loss.

# NOTES

*Epigraphs:* James Stewart, "Eight Days," *New Yorker*, September 21, 2009; F. A. Hayek, *The Fatal Conceit: The Errors of Socialism*, ed. W. W. Bartley III (Chicago: University of Chicago Press, 1988), 76.

## INTRODUCTION

1.  Two very useful overviews of the crisis include Martin Neil Baily, Robert E. Litan, and Matthew S. Johnson, *The Origins of the Financial Crisis*, Fixing Finance Series Paper 3 (Washington, DC: Brookings Institution, November 2008), http://www .brookings.edu/~/media/Files/rc/papers/2008/11_origins _crisis_baily_litan/11_origins_crisis_baily_litan.pdf; and Arnold Kling, *Not What They Had in Mind: A History of Policies That Produced the Financial Crisis of 2008* (Arlington, VA: Mercatus Center, September 2008), http://mercatus.org/publication /not-what-they-had-mind-history-policies-produced-financial -crisis-2008. See also James R. Barth et al., *The Rise and Fall of the U.S. Mortgage and Credit Markets* (Santa Monica, CA: Milken Institute, 2009), http://www.milkeninstitute.org/pdf /Riseandfallexcerpt.pdf. Two prescient analyses that were written without the benefit of hindsight and that influenced my thinking are Gary Stern and Ron Feldman, *Too Big to Fail: The Hazards of Bank Bailouts* (Washington, DC: Brookings Institution, 2004); and Joshua Rosner, "Housing in the New Millennium: A Home Without Equity Is Just a Rental with Debt," working paper, June 29, 2001, http://papers.ssrn.com/sol3 /papers.cfm?abstract_id=1162456.
2.  Mark Jickling, *Causes of the Financial Crisis* (Washington, DC: US Congressional Research Service, 2009), http://assets .opencrs.com/rpts/R40173_20090129.pdf.

3. The Financial Crisis Inquiry Commission is a bipartisan commission created in May 2009 to "examine the causes, domestic and global, of the current financial and economic crisis in the United States." See Financial Crisis Inquiry Commission, "About the Commission," http://www.fcic.gov/about/, for a description of the 22 areas the commission is charged with examining.

4. Quoted in William Cohan, *House of Cards: A Tale of Hubris and Wretched Excess on Wall Street* (New York: Doubleday, 2009), p. 450. The bracketed edit is my own substitution for family consumption.

5. Paul Samuelson, "Don't Expect Recovery Before 2012—With 8% Inflation," interview by Nathan Gardels, *New Perspectives Quarterly* 27 (Spring 2009), http://www.digitalnpq.org /articles/economic/331/01-16-2009/paul_samuelson.

6. Gretchen Morgenson and Don Van Natta Jr., "Paulson's Calls to Goldman Tested Ethics," *New York Times*, August 8, 2009, http://www.nytimes.com/2009/08/09/business/09paulson .html?_r=3&hpw.

7. Here is one tally of Goldman Sachs's revolving door with the government: "A Revolving Door," http://media.mcclatchydc .com/static/images/goldman/20091028_Jobs_GOLDMAN .pdf. See also Kate Kelly and Jon Hilsenrath, "New York Chairman's Ties to Goldman Raise Questions," *Wall Street Journal*, May 4, 2009, http://online.wsj.com/article /SB124139546243981801.html. And one look at the money flows from Wall Street to Washington is "Among Bailout Supporters, Wall St. Donations Ran High," *New York Times*, September 30, 2008, http://dealbook.blogs.nytimes.com /2008/09/30/among-bailout-supporters-wall-st-donations -ran-high.

## 1. GAMBLING WITH OTHER PEOPLE'S MONEY

1. I want to thank Paul Romer for the poker analogy, which is much better than my original idea of using dice. He also provided the quote about the "sucker at the table" that I use later.

2. Many economists, including this one, grossly underestimated the potential impact of the subprime crisis because we did not understand the extent or impact of leverage. Mea culpa.

## 2. DID CREDITORS EXPECT
## TO GET RESCUED?

1.  The policy of government bailout is usually called "too big to fail." But government occasionally lets large financial institutions fail. As I show below, the government almost always makes sure that creditors get all the money they were promised. The rescue of creditors is what creates excessive leverage and removes the incentive of the one group—creditors—with the natural incentive to monitor recklessness.

2.  See Robert L. Hetzel, "Too Big to Fail: Origins, Consequences, and Outlook," *Economic Review* (Nov./Dec. 1991), http://www.richmondfed.org/publications/research/economic_review/1991/er770601.cfm.

3.  C. T. Conover, testimony before the House Subcommittee on Financial Institutions Supervision, Regulation and Insurance of the Committee on Banking, Finance, and Urban Affairs, *Inquiry into Continental Illinois Corp. and Continental Illinois National Bank*, 98th Cong., 2nd sess., 1984, http://fraser.stlouisfed.org/historicaldocs/678/download/63823/house_cinb1984.pdf.

4.  Irvine Sprague, *Bailout: An Insider's Account of Bank Failures and Rescues* (New York: Basic Books, 1986), p. 242.

5.  Stern and Feldman, *Too Big to Fail*, 12. They do not provide data on what proportion of these deposits were uninsured.

6.  See "Predator's Fall: Drexel Burnham Lambert," *Time*, February 26, 1990, http://www.time.com/time/magazine/article/0,9171,969468,00.html.

7.  Charles W. Parker III, "International Investor Influence in the 1994–1995 Mexican Peso Crisis," working paper, Columbia International Affairs Online, Columbia University, 2005, http://www.ciaonet.org/wps/cid096/ (login required).

8.  Willem Buiter quoted by Carl Gewirtz in "Mexico: Why Save Speculators?" *New York Times*, February 2, 1995, http://www.nytimes.com/1995/02/02/business/worldbusiness/02iht-bail.html?scp=13&sq=tesobonos%20mexico%20bailout&st=cse.

9.  See Roger Lowenstein, *When Genius Failed: The Rise and Fall of Long-Term Capital Management* (New York: Random House, 2000).

10. Nell Henderson, "Backstopping the Economy Too Well?" *Washington Post*, June 30, 2005, http://www.washingtonpost

.com/wp-dyn/content/article/2005/06/29/AR2005062902841
.html.

11. See Barry Ritholtz, *Bailout Nation* (New York: Wiley, 2009),
and the following podcast with Ritholtz: Library of Economics
and Liberty, "Ritholtz on Bailouts, the Fed, and the Crisis,"
http://www.econtalk.org/archives/2010/03/ritholtz_on_bai
.html.

12. Investopedia, "Case Study: The Collapse of Lehman
Brothers," http://www.investopedia.com/articles/economics
/09/lehman-brothers-collapse.asp?viewed=1.

13. Buying a credit default swap on Lehman was insurance
against Lehman defaulting on its promises. The fact that the
price fell between March and May in the aftermath of Bear's
collapse means that it was cheaper to buy that insurance.
Evidently traders believed that Lehman was unlikely to go
bankrupt.

14. See Liz Rappaport and Carrick Mollenkamp, "Lehman's
Bonds Find Stability," *Wall Street Journal*, June 13, 2008,
http://online.wsj.com/article/SB121331446000169869.html.
They wrote, "The tempered reaction in the bond markets
underscores investors' conviction the Federal Reserve won't
let a major U.S. securities dealer collapse and that Lehman
Brothers may be ripe for a takeover. In March, when Bear
Stearns was collapsing, protection on Lehman's bonds
cost more than twice as much as it does now." A nice
description of how credit default swaps worked and some
levels they traded at for various firms at different times
is available at http://www.briefing.com/GeneralContent
/Investor/Active/ArticlePopup/ArticlePopup.aspx?ArticleId
=NS20080912145604TankingStock.

15. One prominent exception is John Taylor, who argues that
it was Paulson's panic and apocalyptic threats of disaster
that spooked the markets, not Lehman going bankrupt. See
John Taylor, *Getting off Track: How Government Actions and
Interventions Caused, Prolonged, and Worsened the Financial
Crisis* (Stanford, CA: Hoover Institution Press, 2009).

16. "Lehman Next to Be Squeezed?" *Sydney Morning Herald*,
March 15, 2008, http://www.smh.com.au/business/lehman
-next-to-be-squeezed-20080315-1zme.html.

17. See Figure 7 in James R. Barth, Tong Li, and Triphon
Phumiwasana, "The U.S. Financial Crisis: Credit Crunch and

Yield Spreads," http://www.apeaweb.org/confer/bei08 /papers/blp.pdf.

18. In other words, even as Fannie and Freddie were near death, they were still able to borrow at rates only 1 percent above the rates the US government was offering on Treasuries.

19. See Congressional Budget Office, "CBO's Budgetary Treatment of Fannie Mae and Freddie Mac," background paper, January 2010, pp. 7–8, http://www.cbo.gov/ftpdocs /108xx/doc10878/01-13-FannieFreddie.pdf.

20. John Arlidge, "I'm Doing 'God's Work.' Meet Mr. Goldman Sachs," *Sunday Times*, November 8, 2009, http://www .timesonline.co.uk/tol/news/world/us_and_americas /article6907681.ece?token=null&offset=0&page=1.

21. The Peltzman effect, named for Sam Peltzman's innovative work on automobile safety regulation, is a form of moral hazard. Clive Thompson, "Bicycle Helmets Put You at Risk," *New York Times*, December 10, 2006, offers a fascinating example of subconscious effects. This study finds that drivers drive closer to cyclists when they are wearing a helmet. Wearing a helmet increases the chance of being hit by a car.

22. See the posts at Macroeconomic Resilience, http://www .macroresilience.com, for Hayekian arguments on how moral hazard selects for risk-taking, particularly in the presence of principal–agent problems.

23. Andrew Haldane, "Why Banks Failed the Stress Test," Marcus-Evans Conference on Stress-Testing, February 9–10, 2009, pp. 12–13, http://www.bankofengland.co.uk /publications/speeches/2009/speech374.pdf.

## 4. HEADS—THEY WIN A RIDICULOUSLY ENORMOUS AMOUNT; TAILS—THEY WIN JUST AN ENORMOUS AMOUNT

1. Lucian A. Bebchuk and Holger Spamann, "Regulating Bankers' Pay," *Georgetown Law Journal* 98, no. 2 (2010): 247–287, http://ssrn.com/abstract=1410072.

2. George Akerlof and Paul Romer, "Looting: The Economic Underworld of Bankruptcy for Profit," *Brookings Papers on Economic Activity* 24, no. 2 (1993): 1–74, http://ideas.repec .org/a/bin/bpeajo/v24y1993i1993-2p1-74.html. See also William Black, *The Best Way to Rob a Bank Is to Own One:*

*How Corporate Executives and Politicians Looted the S&L Industry* (Austin: University of Texas Press, 2009).

3. Cohan, *House of Cards*, 90.

4. Cayne sold down from his largest holdings of about seven million shares to six million. Some of those sales presumably took place near the peak of Bear Stearns's value. Others may have occurred on the way down, and, of course, the sale of his six million Bear Stearns shares at the end did net him $61 million.

5. One of the standard explanations for the imprudence of Wall Street was the move from partnerships to publicly traded firms that allowed Wall Street to gamble with other people's money. There is some truth to this explanation, but it ignores the question of why the partnerships were replaced with publicly traded firms. The desire to grow larger and become more leveraged than a partnership would allow was part of the reason, but that desire isn't sufficient. I'd like to be able to borrow from other people to finance my investments, but I can't. Why did it become easier for Wall Street to do so in the late 1980s through the 1990s? Partly because of the increase in the perception that government would rescue lenders to large risk-takers.

6. Mark Maremont, John Hechinger, and Maurice Tamman, "Before the Bust, These CEOs Took Money off the Table," *Wall Street Journal*, November 20, 2008, http://online.wsj.com /article/SB122713829045342487-search.html?KEYWORDS =mark+maremont&COLLECTION=wsjie/6month (subscription required).

7. Ibid.

8. Lucian Bebchuk, Alma Cohen, and Holger Spamann, "The Wages of Failure: Executive Compensation at Bear Stearns and Lehman 2000–2008," working draft, Harvard Law School, November 22, 2009, http://www.law.harvard.edu /faculty/bebchuk/pdfs/BCS-Wages-of-Failure-Nov09.pdf.

## 5. HOW CREDITOR RESCUE AND HOUSING POLICY COMBINED WITH REGULATION TO BLOW UP THE HOUSING MARKET

1. There's a problem with taking out a loan for 103 percent of the price of the house when the price of the house exceeds the value that would be there without the opportunity to get into this lottery. That problem is the appraisal. There

are numerous media accounts of how the appraisal process was corrupted—lenders stopped using honest appraisers and stuck with those who could "hit the target," the selling price. Why would a lender want to inflate the appraised value? Normally they wouldn't. But if you're selling to Fannie or Freddie, you don't have an incentive to be cautious. Andrew Cuomo, the former US Department of Housing and Urban Development (HUD) secretary who increased Fannie and Freddie's affordable housing goals, and currently the attorney general of New York, investigated Washington Mutual and Fannie and Freddie's roles in corrupting the appraisal process. Fannie and Freddie ended up making a $24 million commitment over five years to create an independent appraisal institute. Cuomo has not revealed what he found at Fannie and Freddie that got them to make that commitment. See Kenneth R. Harney, "Fighting Back Against Corrupt Appraisals," *Washington Post*, March 15, 2008, http://www.washingtonpost.com/wp-dyn/content/article /2008/03/14/AR2008031402007.

2. See Taxpayer Relief Act of 1997, Library of Congress, THOMAS, http://thomas.loc.gov/cgi-bin/bdquery/z ?d105:HR02014.

3. Federal Reserve Bank of New York, "Federal Funds Data," http://www.newyorkfed.org/markets/omo/dmm /fedfundsdata.cfm.

4. John Taylor blames poor monetary policy for much of the crisis. See Taylor, *Getting Off Track*. Greenspan's "theya culpa" (in which he blames everyone but himself) can be found in Alan Greenspan, "The Crisis," *Brookings Papers on Economic Activity*, March 9, 2010, http://www.brookings .edu/~/media/Files/Programs/ES/BPEA/2010_spring_bpea _papers/spring2010_greenspan.pdf.

5. See Noelle Knox, "43% of First-Time Home Buyers Put No Money Down," *USA Today*, January 17, 2006; and Daniel H. Mudd, "Remarks at the NAR Regional Summit on Housing Opportunities," Vienna, VA, April 24, 2006.

6. Mudd, "Remarks."

7. This was the growth in the middle tier (the middle one-third by price) in Washington, DC, in the Case-Shiller index for DC: http://www.standardandpoors.com/indices/sp-case-shiller -home-price-indices/en/us/?indexId=spusa-cashpidff–p-us—.

## 6. FANNIE AND FREDDIE

1. William J. Clinton, "Remarks on the National Homeownership Strategy," June 5, 1995, http://www.presidency.ucsb.edu/ws /index.php?pid=51448.
2. George W. Bush, "Remarks on Signing the American Dream Downpayment Act," December 16, 2003, http://www .presidency.ucsb.edu/ws/index.php?pid=64935.
3. Roger Lowenstein, "Who Needs the Mortgage-Interest Deduction?" *New York Times*, March 5, 2006, http://www .nytimes.com/2006/03/05/magazine/305deduction.1.html? _r=2&pagewanted=print.
4. I want to thank Arnold Kling, who helped me understand the workings of the banks, the housing market, and the rationale for Fannie and Freddie in this podcast: Library of Economics and Liberty, "Kling on Freddie and Fannie and the Recent History of the U.S. Housing Market," http://www.econtalk.org /archives/2008/09/kling_on_freddi.html.
5. See, for example, Paul Krugman, "Fannie, Freddie and You," *New York Times*, July 14, 2008, http://www.nytimes.com /2008/07/14/opinion/14krugman.html?_r=2&oref=slogin.
6. See Theresa R. DiVenti, "Fannie Mae and Freddie Mac: Past, Present, and Future," *Cityscape: A Journal of Policy Development and Research* 11, no. 3 (2009). Between 2001 and 2005, Fannie and Freddie purchases of single-family mortgages hit all-time highs—over $900 billion in each year and over $2 trillion in 2003. In each of those years, 5 percent of Fannie Mae's volume was loans with credit scores below 620. Another 10 percent or more were between 620 and 660. Freddie Mac's numbers were almost as large. In 2003, Fannie and Freddie purchased $285 billion of single-family loans with credit scores below 660. By 2008, Fannie Mae alone was holding $345 billion of Alt-A loans. See Maurna Desmond, "Fannie's Alt-A Issue," *Forbes*, May 6, 2008, http://www.forbes.com/2008/05/06/fannie-mae -closer2-markets-equity-cx_md_0506markets50.html. Below, I detail Fannie and Freddie's involvement in low down pay- ment loans.
7. Alistar Barr, "Fannie Mae Could Be Hit Hard by Housing Bust: Berg," *MarketWatch*, September 18, 2006, http://www .marketwatch.com/story/fannie-mae-could-lose-29-bln-in -housing-bust-hedge-firm.

8. Joseph Stiglitz, *The Roaring Nineties: A New History of the World's Most Prosperous Decade* (New York: W. W. Norton and Company, 2004), pp. 104–105, http://books.google.com /books?id=yxhV44nSN_4C&printsec=frontcover&dq=Joseph +Stiglitz,+The+Roaring+Nineties:+A+New+History+of+the +World%E2%80%99s+Most+Prosperous+Decade&source=bl &ots=O9HdPQven7&sig=95Fh7OkZa4eDK5E7ax1y6kRCZ10 &hl=en&ei=SZKyS8O6BInQtAO098HMBA&sa=X&oi=book _result&ct=result&resnum=1&ved=0CAYQ64AEwAA#v =onepage&q=&f=false.

9. Office of Federal Housing Enterprise Oversight, *2008 Report to Congress* (Washington, DC: OFHEO, 2008), http://www .fhfa.gov/webfiles/2097/OFHEOReporttoCongress2008.pdf.

10. US Department of Housing and Urban Development (HUD), "HUD Prepares to Set New Housing Goals," *U.S. Housing Market Conditions Summary* (Summer 1998), http://www .huduser.org/Periodicals/ushmc/summer98/summary-2 .html#note5.

11. HUD, "Overview of the GSEs' Housing Goal Performance, 1993–2001," http://www.huduser.org/Datasets/GSE/gse2001 .pdf.

12. HUD, "Overview of the GSEs' Housing Goal Performance, 2000–2007," http://www.huduser.org/Datasets/GSE/gse2007 .pdf.

13. Neither GSE reached the 2008 goal of 56 percent: the party was over.

14. Federal National Mortgage Association (Fannie Mae), *2002 Annual Housing Activities Report*, March 17, 2003, p. 12, http://www.fhfa.gov/webfiles/382/HMG_MAE_-_2002 _AHAR.pdf.

15. Jay Romano, "Your Home: Lowering Mortgage Barriers," *New York Times*, October 20, 2002, http://www.nytimes .com/2002/10/20/realestate/your-home-lowering-mortgage -barriers.html?pagewanted=all.

16. "CitiMortgage and Fannie Mae Announce $100 Billion Affordable Housing Alliance," *Business Wire*, October 29, 2003, http://www.allbusiness.com/banking-finance/banking -lending-credit-services/5774550-1.html.

17. See John W. Straka, "A Shift in the Mortgage Landscape: The 1990s Move to Automated Credit Evalutions," *Journal of Housing Research* 11, no. 2 (2000).

18. Gary Crum, "Get Fast Loan Approaval," *Christian Science Monitor*, July 3, 2000, http://www.csmonitor.com/2000/0703 /p16s2.html.

19. HUD, "HUD Prepares to Set New Housing Goals," http://www .huduser.org/Periodicals/ushmc/summer98/summary-2.html.

20. Franklin Raines, testimony before the House Committee of Financial Services, *Hearing on H.R. 2575, the Secondary Mortgage Market Enterprises Regulatory Improvement Act*, 108th Cong., 1st sess., 2003, http://financialservices.house .gov/media/pdf/092503fr.pdf.

21. These figures on the loan-to-value ratio are taken from HUD, "Profiles of GSE Mortgage Purchases," Tables 10a and 10b, http://www.huduser.org/portal/datasets/gse.html.

22. One reason that piggybacks supplant PMI during this period is that the piggyback loan's Interest is tax deductible. Starting in 2007, PMI became tax deductible.

23. See Eric Rosengren, "Current Challenges in Housing and Home Loans: Complicating Factors and Implications for Policymakers," paper presented at the New England Economic Partnership's Spring Economic Outlook Conference, Boston, MA, May 30, 2008, figure 11, http://www.bos.frb.org/news /speeches/rosengren/2008/053008.pdf.

24. For on-the-ground examples of the incentives facing lenders and homebuilders, see Alyssa Katz, *Our Lot: How Real Estate Came to Own Us* (New York: Bloomsbury USA, 2009). Katz also gives an excellent overview of the myriad political forces pushing homeownership.

25. Sam Eddins, director of research at IronBridge Capital Management, pointed out to me that the cause of the spread between GSE bonds and Treasuries was not so much due to the uncertainty over whether the government would indeed rescue the GSEs in the event of default, but rather the dif-ferential tax status of Treasuries versus GSE bonds. Treasuries are exempt from state and local taxes while GSE bonds are not.

## 7. FANNIE AND FREDDIE—CAUSE OR EFFECT?

1. Many have argued that Fannie and Freddie couldn't be the cause of the housing bubble because many other coun-tries had housing bubbles, but they didn't have Fannie and Freddie. But the United States is not the only country that

pushed homeownership via national policy initiatives. The full story of the global housing market has yet to be told. For an argument that monetary policy errors are correlated with housing bubbles around the world, see Rudiger Ahrend, Boris Cournede, and Robert Price, "Monetary Policy, Market Excesses and Financial Turmoil," *OECD Economics Department Working Papers, No. 597* (2008), http://www.sourceoecd.org/rpsv/cgi-bin/wppdf?file=5kzpp5qcghg0.pdf.

2. See Carol Leonnig, "How HUD Mortgage Policy Helped Fuel the Crisis," *Washington Post*, June 10, 2008, http://www.washingtonpost.com/wp-dyn/content/article/2008/06/09/AR2008060902626.html.

3. They were also an important part of the Community Reinvestment Act's (CRA) impact on the price of real estate in low-income areas. The CRA was not an important cause of the crisis, but it contributed by helping to drive up the demand for real estate in low-income areas. Fannie and Freddie were deeply entangled with the CRA, making it difficult to measure any independent effect of CRA. That entanglement included Fannie and Freddie guaranteeing securitized CRA loans and direct purchases of CRA loans to make them more palatable to the banks and to meet Fannie and Freddie's housing goals. See Wachovia, "First Union Capital Markets Corp., Bear, Stearns & Co. Price Securities Offering Backed by Affordable Mortgages," Press Release, October 20, 1997, https://www.wachovia.com/foundation/v/index.jsp?vgnextoid=dde12e3d3471f110VgnVCM200000627d6fa2RCRD&crd&vgnextfmt=default&key_guid=52e84a86591eb110VgnVCM100000ca0d1872RCRD; and Jamie S. Gorelick, "Remarks," American Bankers Association National Community and Economic Development Conference, October 30, 2000, http://web.archive.org/web/20011120061407/www.fanniemae.com/news/speeches/speech_152.html.

4. Stuart Gabriel and Stuart Rosenthal find no evidence of crowd-out between 1994 and 2003 (the GSEs had a real impact on credit availability) but do find crowd-out between 2004 and 2006. See "Do the GSEs Expand the Supply of Mortgage Credit? New Evidence of Crowd Out in the Secondary Mortgage Market," paper prepared for the National Association of Realtors, December 2, 2009, http://faculty.maxwell.syr.edu/rosenthal/Recent%20Papers

/Gabriel-Rosenthal-GSE%20Purchase%20Goals%20and%20
Crowd%20Out%20-%2012-2-09.pdf.

5.  See Jonas D. M. Fisher and Saad Quayyum, "The Great Turn-
of-the-Century Housing Boom," *Economic Perspectives*
30, no. 3 (Third Quarter 2006), http://ssrn.com/abstract
=925280; and Atif R. Mian and Amir Sufi, "The Consequences
of Mortgage Credit Expansion: Evidence from the U.S.
Mortgage Default Crisis," working paper, December 12, 2008,
http://ssrn.com/abstract=1072304.

6.  In 2003, a National Association of Realtors survey found that
28 percent of all first-time homebuyers bought their homes
with no money down. See Sarah Max, "Home Buying with No
Money Down," CNNMoney.com, December 23, 2003, http://
money.cnn.com/2003/12/23/pf/yourhome/nodownpayment
/index.htm. By 2005, that number was 43 percent. The
median first-time homebuyer put 2 percent down. See Noelle
Knox, "43% of First-Time Buyers Put No Money Down,"
USAToday.com, January 17, 2006, http://www.usatoday
.com/money/perfi/housing/2006-01-17-real-estate-usat_x
.htm. See also National Association of Realtors, "Profile of
Home Buyers and Sellers," http://www.realtor.org/research
/research/reportsbuysell. Who funded those mortgages?
Fannie and Freddie funded some but not all of them. Who
funded the rest? How many were securitized privately? It
would be useful to know.

## 8. COMMERCIAL BANKS AND INVESTMENT BANKS

1.  Nassim Nicholas Taleb, in discussion with the author for
EconTalk, March 23, 2009, http://www.econtalk.org/archives
/2009/03/taleb_on_the_fi.html.

2.  Riccardo Rebonato, *The Plight of the Fortune Tellers: Why
We Need to Manage Financial Risk Differently* (Princeton, NJ:
Princeton University Press, 2007).

## 9. PICKING UP NICKELS

1.  See Macroeconomic Resilience, "A 'Rational' Explanation
of the Financial Crisis," working paper, 2009, http://www
.macroresilience.com/wp-content/uploads/2009/11/A
-Rational-Explanation-of-the-Financial-Crisis.pdf, for an

explanation of the attractiveness of negative skewness—payoffs where there is a high probability of a small positive return and a small probability of catastrophic losses. Small returns are unpleasant, but enough leverage makes them tolerable. And as long as the catastrophe doesn't materialize for a while, you can look prudent and respectable playing the game.

2. This helps explain the seemingly absurd explosion in the synthetic CDO market and the credit default swap market. Once Wall Street figured out how to manufacture AAA-rated securities, it was inevitable that someone would get flattened.

## 10. BASEL—FAULTY

1. For more information on Basel II, see Board of Governors of the Federal Reserve System, "Basel Regulatory Framework," http://www.federalreserve.gov/GeneralInfo/basel2.

2. See Marty Rosenblatt, "U.S. Banking Agencies Approve Final Rule on Recourse and Residuals," *Speaking of Securitization* 6, no. 4 (December 5, 2001), http://www.securitization.net /pdf/dt_recourse_120501.pdf.

3. Some say a change in capital requirements in 2004 that allowed the broker-dealer part of investment banks to become more leveraged "caused" the crisis. See Stephen Labaton, "Agency's '04 Rule Let Banks Pile Up New Debt," *New York Times*, October 2, 2008. It may have contributed, but as far as I can tell from the press and conversations with insiders, the holding companies of the investment banks were essentially on their own with respect to how much capital they chose to hold, and that was more important. The investment banks were also affected by the 2005 European regulations that encouraged the use of VaR. Despite numerous off-the-record conversations with insiders, I've struggled to figure out exactly how these regulations changed the incentives facing investment banks. What is clear is how unclear the regulatory world of investment banks is to those of us on the outside.

## 11. WHERE DO WE GO FROM HERE?

1. Milton Friedman and Rose Friedman, *Free to Choose* (Orlando, FL: Harcourt Books, 1980), p. 45.

2. I discuss this in more detail in "How Little We Know," *Economists' Voice* (November 2009), http://www .invisibleheart.com/How%20Little%20We%20Know.pdf.

3. Milton Friedman, "Why It Isn't Necessary to 'Throw the Bums Out,'" video file from a speech circa 1977, http://www .youtube.com/watch?v=ac9j15eig_w&feature=related.

# INDEX

Parker, Charles, 15
Paulson, Hank, 3, 80, 88n15
Peltzman, Sam, 89n21
piggyback loan, 55–57, 61, 94n22
*Plight of the Fortune Tellers, The*
(Rebonato), 66–67
poker, analogy with, 7–8, 70, 86n1
bailouts in, 14, 17
commercial, investment banks
in, 63–64
executives in, 27
government in, 9–11
housing market in, 35–36
mortgage-backed securities
in, 69
politicians, government-
sponsored enterprises and,
47, 49–50, 52, 54, 61
private mortgage insurance
(PMI), 55–57, 94n22
profitability, of bailouts, xvi
publicly traded firms, 90n5

Raines, Frank, 53–55
ratings agencies, 74
Reagan, Ronald, 2
Rebonato, Riccardo, 66–67
reform
difficulty of, 78
recommendations for, 78–81
rescue. *See* bailouts
Reserve Primary, 18–19
risk. *See also* Value at Risk
assessment models of, 66–67
of bank executives, 27–33
equity holders and, 25–26
Gaussian distributions of, 32
of government-sponsored
enterprises, 20–21, 26,
89n18

moral hazard and, 89n22
of publicly traded firms, 90n5
*Roaring Nineties, The* (Stiglitz),
46
Romer, Paul, 29, 86n1
Rosenthal, Stuart, 95n4
Royal Bank of Scotland (RBS),
66–67

Samuelson, Paul, 2
savings and loan (S&L) crisis,
14, 29
Schwartz, Alan, 1
Securities and Exchange
Commission, 47
Spamann, Holger, 27–28, 32
Sprague, Irvine, 14
Stiglitz, Joseph, 46
stress-testing, 22–23
subprime crisis, 65f. *See also*
financial crisis
commercial banks role in,
62–65
economists underestimating,
86n2
extreme leverage and, 11, 35
government-sponsored
enterprises role in, 44–45,
50, 59–61, 63–65, 92n6, 94n1
investment banks role in,
62–68
risk assessment models and,
66–67

Taleb, Nassim Nicholas, xv
tax policy
GSE bonds and, 94n25
housing market and, 37,
94n22
Taxpayer Relief Act of 1997, 37

# ABOUT THE AUTHOR

Russ Roberts is the John and Jean De Nault Research Fellow at Stanford University's Hoover Institution. Roberts hosts the weekly podcast EconTalk—hour-long conversations with authors, economists, psychologists, historians, and philosophers. Past guests include Milton Friedman, Thomas Piketty, Nassim Nicholas Taleb, Christopher Hitchens, Marc Andreessen, Martha Nussbaum, Mariana Mazzucato, Michael Pollan, and Bill James. Over 650 episodes are available at EconTalk.org and on iTunes at no charge.

His two rap videos on the ideas of John Maynard Keynes and F.A. Hayek, created with filmmaker John Papola, have had more than ten million views on YouTube. His animated poem, It's a Wonderful Loaf, an ode to the emergent order of our everyday lives, can be found at wonderfulloaf.org. His video series on the pitfalls of data and the American economy is "The Numbers Game" and can be found at Policyed.org.

His latest book is *How Adam Smith Can Change Your Life: An Unexpected Guide to Human Nature and Happiness* (Portfolio/Penguin 2014). It takes the lessons from Adam Smith's little-known masterpiece *The Theory of Moral Sentiments* and applies them to modern life.

He is also the author of three economic novels teaching economic lessons and ideas through fiction. *The Price of Everything: A Parable of Possibility and Prosperity* (Princeton University Press, 2008), *The Invisible Heart: An Economic Romance* (MIT Press, 2002), and *The Choice: A Fable of Free Trade and Protectionism* (Prentice Hall, 3rd edition, 2006). *The Choice* was named one of the top ten books of 1994 by Business Week and one of the best books of 1994 by the Financial Times.

Roberts archives his work at russroberts.info and writes at Medium.com. His twitter handle is @econtalker.